Endorsements

"I was fully engaged right from the opening words. Dionne writes with incredible transparency and her testimony is compelling. It will be an encouragement to many. The Art of Freedom will meet a lot of people right where they are living!"
—*Gary J. Blanchard*
Assistant Superintendent and Executive Secretary Illinois District Council Assemblies of God
Carlinville, Illinois

"Truly *awesome*. Well written, meaningful, easy to read and comprehend! The Art of Freedom will make a great small group study."
—*Anna Simon*
Author of "Kimberly's Flight", Freelance Writer for Clemson University and Career Long Journalist for the Greenville News in Greenville, SC
Pawleys Island, SC

The Art of Freedom

Restore Your Heart, Renew Your Soul, and Revive Your Body to Live Transformed

Dionne White

The Art of Freedom © 2020 by Dionne White. All rights reserved.
Printed in the United States of America
Published by Author Academy Elite
PO Box 43, Powell, OH 43035
www.AuthorAcademyElite.com

All rights reserved. This book contains material protected under International and Federal Copyright Laws and Treaties. Any unauthorized reprint or use of this material is prohibited. No part of this book may be reproduced or transmitted in any form or by any means, electronic or mechanical, including photocopying, recording, or by any information storage and retrieval system, without express written permission from the author.

Identifiers:
LCCN: 2020902750
ISBN: 978-1-64746-147-8 (paperback)
ISBN: 978-1-64746-148-5 (hardback)
ISBN: 978-1-64746-149-2 (ebook)

Available in paperback, hardback, e-book, and audiobook

Unless otherwise indicated, all scripture quotations are taken from the Holy Bible, New Kings James Version®, Copyright ©1982 by Thomas Nelson. Used by permission. All rights reserved.

Scripture quotations marked are taken from the NASB are from the New American Standard Bible, Copyright ©1960, 1962, 1963, 1968, 1971, 1972, 1973, 1975, 1977, 1995 by The Lockman Foundation.

Used by permission. (www.Lockman.org)

Scripture quotations marked KJV are from the
King James Version of the Bible.

Scripture quotations marked NIV®. Copyright © 1973, 1978, 1984, 2011 by Biblica, Inc.TM Used by permission of Zondervan. All rights reserved worldwide. (www.biblehub.com)

Scripture quotations marked NLT are from the Holy Bible, New Living Translation, Copyright ©1996, 2004, 2007. Used by permission of Tyndale House Publishers, Inc. Wheaton, IL 60189. All rights reserved.

Scripture quotations marked AMP are from the Amplified Bible. Copyright© 1954, 1958, 1962, 1964, 1965, 1987 by The Lockman Foundation. Used by permission.

Scripture quotations are from the ESV® Bible (The Holy Bible, English Standard Version®), Copyright© 2001 by Crossway Bibles, a publishing ministry of Good News Publishers. Used by permission. All rights reserved.

Scripture quotations marked CSB are the Christian Standard Bible®, Copyright© 2017 by Holman Bible Publishers. Used by permission. Christian Standard Bible® and CSB® are federally registered trademarks of Holman Bible Publishers.

Word definitions used by permission of NavPress Publishing Group, by Vine's Concise Dictionary of Bible Words W.E. Vine, Thomas Nelson Publishers Copyright ©1985, 1980

Word Definitions used by permission of Strong's Exhaustive Concordance of the Bible with Hebrew Aramaic and Greek Dictionaries Copyright © 1981, 1998 by The Lockman Foundation, All rights reserved Lockman.org (biblehub.com)

Word definitions used by permission of Merriam-Webster Collegiate Dictionary, 11th ed., Merriam-Webster, updated and expanded edition, Merriam-Webster, Incorporated, Copyright ©1982, 2003 at www.merriam-webster.com

Word definitions used by permission of Any Internet addresses (websites, blogs, etc.) and telephone numbers printed in this book are offered as a resource. They are not intended in any way to be or imply an endorsement by Author Academy Elite, nor does Author Academy Elite vouch for the content of these sites and numbers for the life of this book.

Book design by JETLAUNCH. Cover design by Debbie O'Byrne.

Dedication

This book is dedicated first and foremost to God, the Father, Son, and Holy Spirit. It is because of Jesus Christ, my Savior, my Redeemer, my Healer, and the Restorer of the Ruins, that I am able to write this book. Without Him there would be no story or book. He *restored* my heart, *renewed* my soul, and *revived* my body, giving me new life, joy, peace, purpose, and a burning fire to know Him and to make Him known.

In addition, I dedicate this book to my faithful and incredible husband and two children. They chose to stand by me in faith, encouragement, joy, and love. They, like Jesus, believed in me and never gave up on me. To my husband, Will, thank you for being a rock and a light with your devotion and dedication to me as a husband, friend, caretaker, and provider in the seasons when my faith wore thin. You are a godly man of integrity with a heart of service that is a testimony and act of sacrifice every day. Thank you for believing in me and the powerful message of *The Art of Freedom*. I am forever grateful.

Last, but not least, I dedicate this book to my parents and family members for always standing by me through every season of life, loving me the best that they knew how, and believing in me as an artist, friend, and mother. To my dad, Louis DiFabio, for instilling in me a thirst for knowledge, truth, teaching, justice, patriotism, and hard work. Thank you for being a role model of integrity and strength.

Special Remembrance

I am thankful to my beloved late mother, Gloria Jean Kostella Di Fabio. Her effervescent and vibrant spirit was a gift and light in a dark world. She lit up rooms with her smile and piano playing. She always saw the sunny side of life, and believed in me and my gift of art. She devoted herself to raising and praying for her children, and encouraged me to keep the faith. It was her desire that I would return to my art and use my gifts to bless others and glorify God. Words cannot describe my love for my mother and how I wish she were here to share this milestone with me. As she would say, *"*You have it, produce it.*"* How right she was. Until we meet again, Mom, I will keep creating, keep the faith, and live it with a song in my heart.

CONTENTS

Acknowledgments..................................xiii
Note to the Reader xv
Contributors.................................... xvii
Disclaimer xix

Part 1:
The Art of Freedom: God Encounters

Chapter 1: A Modern-Day Egypt.................... 3
Chapter 2: Displaying His Glory................... 12
Chapter 3: The Night the Veil Lifted 19
Chapter 4: I'm Healing You....................... 27
Chapter 5: Vision Births Hope 33

Part 2:
The Art of Restoring the Heart: Humility, Surrender, and Forgiveness

Chapter 6: The Art of Restoring the Heart........... 45
Chapter 7: The Art of Generational Freedom 52

Chapter 8: The Art of Surrender 57

Chapter 9: The Art of Getting Up 62

PART 3:
THE ART OF RENEWING THE SOUL:
BE TRANSFORMED BY RENEWING YOUR MIND

Chapter 10: The Art of Renewing the Mind 71

Chapter 11: The Art of Possessing Peace 76

Chapter 12: The Art of Being Transformed 82

Chapter 13: The Art of Being Online 90

Chapter 14: The Art of Guarding Your Gate 99

Chapter 15: The Art of Not Going Back 104

PART 4:
THE ART OF REVIVING THE BODY:
LET YOUR KINGDOM COME IN ME

Chapter 16: The Art of Reviving the Body 111

Chapter 17: The Art of Rest 120

Chapter 18: The Art of Painting the Promise 134

Chapter 19: The Art of Kintsugi 142

Endnotes 155

About the Author 157

A Note to Creatives 159

ACKNOWLEDGMENTS

There are many who stepped up and blessed my life in one way or another on my spiritual, emotional, physical, and creative journey. I am thankful for them all, and I truly cannot repay them for their kindness and support.

I want to acknowledge my dear friend and editor, Anna Simon. This manuscript became a finished product with her experience and expertise. Thank you for using your gifts to bless me and for being a sounding board and second set of eyes! Thank you for believing in me and my message, *The Art of Freedom*.

God places people in our lives at the most critical time of need, and Theresa Allen was one of those people. Theresa Allen, PhD, and Licensed Professional Counselor at The Well Life, was a key to accelerating my spiritual transformation journey. To Theresa, I am grateful for your ability to see the gold in others and for the way you spoke truth in love to my identity. Thank you for helping me see my worth in Christ again. You were an integral part of helping me bloom after the rain.

NOTE TO THE READER

Welcome to The Art of Freedom. You are in for an exciting, intriguing, healing, and sometimes humorous ride. I am convinced that you did not purchase or receive this book by chance. I believe it is a divine appointment for you and that you are about to embark on a journey that will mark your life with supernatural transformation. As you proceed forward, I just want to share with you a little insight about freedom and destiny.

Freedom and God designed destiny brings warfare. When you are in a cell there is no need for the enemy to attack or go after you, he already has you where he wants you. Satan will just continue to feed you with the "right" food to keep you there; bound, broken, deceived, and defeated.

As the Light begins to stream in you will be awakened and recognize your identity and authority in Christ, realizing you are a much-loved child of God. As you follow the Light and you rise from the prison of ruins moving forward, embracing freedom, it is then that Satan will fight and come in resistance. He does not want you free and able to fulfill the destiny God planned for you. When you become free, he will continue to try and put you back into chains, placing old yokes of bondage upon you with hopes of returning you to your cell. It is right here that I encourage you to fight past the thorns of the past and present to obtain your birthright as a child of God. Be sober, alert and vigilant as you walk in your freedom and protect it.

The Art of Freedom could be a lifesaving and life transforming resource if you approach these pages with an open heart, open mind, and willingness to apply the insight, wisdom, knowledge and practices to your life. I am confident your spirit and mind will be awakened, unlocked, and set on a path to peace, purpose and total transformation! May The Art of Freedom, my personal transformation story, release you into your God given identity, gifts, passions, and purposes for His glory!

9 He who has ears, let him hear."

16 But blessed are your eyes, because they see; and your ears, because they hear. 17 For truly I say to you that many prophets and righteous men desired to see what you see, and did not see it, and to hear what you hear, and did not hear it. 23 And the one on whom seed was sown on the good soil, this is the man who hears the word and understands it; who indeed bears fruit and brings forth, some a hundredfold, some sixty, and some thirty.

—Matthew 13:9,16-17,23 NASB

CONTRIBUTORS

The following have supported me and The Art of Freedom book in one or several of the following ways:

Financially, Spiritually, Emotionally, Story Content, Author and Publishing Coaching, Professional Services of Editing and Proofing.

Toni Wesner
Jan Glazar
Sherry Johnson
Victoria Jimenez
Rachelle Perron-Passwaters
Darla Stitzlein
Wendy Bryant
Anna Simon
Debbie Dalhouse
Igniting Souls Author Coaches
Author Academy Elite Publishing Team

DISCLAIMER

The contents of The Art of Freedom book are for informational purposes only. The content is not intended to be a substitute for professional medical advice, diagnosis, or treatment. The reader should regularly consult a physician or professional licensed counselor in matters relating to his/her physical or mental health and particularly with respect to any symptoms that may require diagnosis or medical attention.

For the mind set on the flesh is death, but the mind set on the Spirit is life and peace.

—Romans 8:6, NASB

PART ONE

The Art of Freedom: God Encounters

Chapter 1
A Modern-Day Egypt

There Is Hope!

Egypt is not a country we live in but a country that lives within us.

—Pope Shenouda III, Egyptian Clergyman 1923-2012

There is a war over our souls. A fight for what is good and right against what is evil and twisted. One way is the path to life, and the other the way of destruction and death. I was living proof that a spirit and soul divided could not live in the fullness and wholeness of God. It wasn't until my mind lined up with my heart that I began to see breakthroughs and experience true whole-person freedom. But it would be almost two decades from when I first said "yes" to Jesus that it would happen. I knew deep within me that God had good plans for me and my life; therefore, I persevered with an inner grit to take hold of that prize.

We are wired to win and be seekers in life. We are wired for love with a desire to win. Our soul longs to be filled and only God can fill that void. We depend on those who raise us and trust them to teach us the things that will help us thrive. Unfortunately, due to the fall of man in the Garden of Eden, the desires of our flesh become stronger as we grow if they are left unharnessed and unchanged by the Spirit of God. Just like Eve, we are tempted by deception and begin to reason and justify our way through life. God's desire was that we would live in Paradise; but unfortunately, that was taken from this earth. Thankfully, now Paradise can live within us when we give our lives to Jesus Christ and surrender to the work of the Holy Spirit. We don't have to just "hold on until we get to heaven"; heaven can live within us right now! That is some Good News!

I was raised in a loving, devoted European-American Roman Catholic home and baptized as a baby. I received my first communion at age six and was confirmed when I was seventeen. I wasn't exactly sure what it all meant at the time. I attended the classes and went through the motions but something kept me from understanding it in its fullness.

There was a battle over my soul and a veil over my mind that kept me from true comprehension. By the time I graduated high school I had become sexually active as I looked for identity, acceptance, and love. My soul was filled with worldly things and carnal desires. My parents made their best effort to love and raise me morally right, but I secretly and openly rebelled. Despite my wayward lifestyle choices, the Lord continued to pursue me.

One Saturday afternoon in the fall of 1990, a friend asked me to go with her to confession. I thought, "Why not?" I definitely had things to confess. A large sin weighed on my soul. The sanctuary was empty when we arrived. The priest was waiting in the confessional. My friend went into the confessional first. I sat down in the middle of the sanctuary and scanned the room to see the dark confessional booths on the side of the aisles. It was daunting. I was extremely nervous and grew more terrified to voice my sin to the man behind the screen. My sin—sexual impurity had led to an abortion, which would be multiplied one year from then to two abortions. I was mortified and overwhelmed with guilt and shame. More than that, I was experiencing an unbelievable presence of fear. I had never known fear and shame like this before. I felt I had secretly brought shame to the family name. Little did I know that Father God saw and knew everything, for He is El Roi, the God who sees me.

As I sat alone on the hard, cold pew, I looked up. In the front of the altar was a statue of Jesus with arms open wide. As I looked at His eyes and open arms, sadness and remorse filled my heart. He knew why I was there. I began to cry and confessed out loud, "Jesus, I am so sorry. I am so sorry for what I have done. I do not want to go in there and tell that man my sin! Please don't make me go in there. Jesus, please forgive me; I never intended for it to be like this. I am so sorry for taking a life that was not mine to take. Please forgive me!" At that moment I felt a warm liquid run down my scalp. It was so real that I reached up to feel it; but there wasn't anything physically there. I whispered, "What is that?" and heard the Lord say, "You are forgiven. I am washing you white as snow. You are forgiven." His blood had covered those murderous acts for me. I felt His amazing grace and forgiveness.

Tears flooded my face and with gratitude I cried, "Thank you Jesus." He responded, "You do not have to go in there." Joy filled my heart and I began to laugh and continued to thank Him! I couldn't believe it; I had just encountered the Living God, and I was laughing in the middle of an empty Catholic sanctuary. My friend came out, sat down next to me, and let out a big sigh. She saw I was laughing and crying and asked me what had happened. I said emphatically, "I don't have to go in there now! I do not have to go in there!" as I pointed at the confessional. I told her what happened, and in a disappointed voice she said, "I wish I had stayed out here"; and we burst out laughing. I felt so free and light. I did not go into the confessional that day nor have I gone into one since. The

God encounter sent me on a pursuit of peace and love. Little did I know He was pursuing me! I began to search for who Jesus really was and how that fit into my life. It would be five years before I was fully convicted by the Holy Spirit and led to intentionally ask the Lord Jesus into my life, making my conversion complete. After that encounter, I was determined to find and understand this walk called Christianity. I knew there had to be more than religious tradition, rules, and regulations. It was undeniable that the Lord was leading me to Him. He faithfully placed people of faith in my path. I was introduced to different Christian denominations that I didn't even know existed, and it excited my spirit. The encounter built my faith in God, but I would soon realize that what I confessed that day would steal my voice and self-worth for years to come.

The Art of Freedom is my story of how God rescued and redeemed me through His passionate pursuit of love for me, revealing my true identity in Him, and radically renewing and transforming me through the power of the cross, His Word and the presence of the Holy Spirit. You will read in the chapters to come how healing and transformation came when I humbled myself, gave up, and allowed the Lord to help me forgive myself and others—ultimately teaching me how to love the woman He designed me to be.

I walk you through some of my most personal God encounter moments, as well as painful memories of my past that led me to find Jesus, my treasure and purpose. I was terrified to let God into those places; but when I did, compassion came instead of condemnation—and that is what I pray will happen for you. May my story of determination and perseverance give you the courage to start and embrace your journey to freedom. I am determined to share His transforming power of truth and love in order to expose and demolish the works of the enemy and help set others free. I write this for His glory!

A friend, not in church at the time, asked me to accompany her to church because her pre-school son had asked to go to school on Sunday, unaware it was a worship service. I told her I would go to support her. At this time, I worked at an optometrist's office with my friend Becki. She was patient, kind, and always encouraging. One day she unobtrusively gave me a Bible tract on being born again. I had no idea what that meant; and it sat on my desk for some time. I finally asked her to explain it to me. I left that day with better knowledge of what born-again salvation was about, but I didn't see how it fit into my life. My friend's three-year-old son and Becki would soon become important puzzle pieces in my salvation story.

Sunday came. The church parking lot was buzzing with people. Joy and hope filled the air. We went inside and up the stairs. I was met by a greeter—Becki, wearing a big smile. To my surprise, her father was the pastor. I was not yet aware of how God orchestrated things like this in our life. I chalked it up to coincidence. I would return to that church with my friends for weeks to come.

On the third visit, the Lord called my name and I couldn't deny it. We were in the back row clapping and singing as Pastor Gary led us in the song "Power in the Blood." This was new to me, as I was brought up Catholic in a more subdued and traditional church atmosphere. The room was small but packed. Pastor Gary sang while his wife Anne played piano and Becki shifted overheads for us to follow along with the songs. It felt good to be in a joyful place. I felt loved there. I felt like I belonged.

Pastor Gary moved across the front with zeal and eventually shed his coat and loosened his tie from the holy heat in the room. After the sermon, Pastor Gary gave the invitation to come to the altar. I gripped the pew tightly, trying to deny the call, but a strong tug on my heart pulled me forward like a marionette on a string. I headed to the altar. Pastor Gary led me through the revelation of my need for a Savior with repentance and acceptance of salvation. I knelt and wept. I had been born again! My friends rejoiced with me, especially Becki.

Saved but Still Walking Wounded

Ten years later, although I was saved, my poor relationship with food was surfacing and my low self-worth brought me to a physical and emotional crisis. I had become severely sleep deprived, depressed, and physically depleted. I couldn't think straight and I ached all over. I went to a doctor who diagnosed me with fibromyalgia and complications from depression and insomnia. I felt like I was entering a slow death and grieved at losing the life I knew. The doctor tried to console me. He said, "There is no cure but there is hope." I felt something leap inside me when he said the word "hope." That was a word I knew. A seed of hope was planted, but it took ten years to produce the fruit of a whole and well life. I sought to understand how to live in true freedom, the freedom that Christ Jesus died to give me. This began my journey to restoring my heart, renewing my soul, and reviving my body.

Through those years several doctors told me to accept and celebrate the "new Dee" because life would just be different now. But this was not the "new Dee" I wanted to celebrate or embrace. In this new mentality, I didn't feel alive; I was simply surviving. Sleep deprivation and multiple medications fogged my thinking; and my will to fight began to slip away as I received diagnosis after diagnosis. I was living the scripture "Hope deferred makes the heart sick." But I wanted the second part of that verse to be my reality: "but when the desire comes, it is a tree of life" (Proverbs 13:12, NKJV).

The Holy Spirit would come and reassure me to keep believing God's word. I began a relentless pursuit to find answers and position myself for healing. I had to find a way out of a maze of long dark corridors—some that led to life and some to dead ends. When faced with disappointment and discouragement, I would lose hope for awhile but I had to find my way out. There was only one way. I knew this, but from my perspective, the way was fuzzy and my focus was still off. I was praying for and seeking the healing instead of fully seeking, knowing, and understanding the Healer. We must seek the Healer. Healing is a promise and it is for us today.

> If you diligently heed the voice of the LORD your God and do what is right in His sight, give ear to His commandments and keep all His statures, I will put none of the diseases on you which I have brought on the Egyptians. For I am the LORD who heals you.
> —Exodus 15:26, NKJV

Sick and Tired of Being Sick and Tired!

You are not your Grandmother!

> I shall not die, but live, and declare the works of the Lord.
> —Psalm 118:17, NKJV

Visits to doctors, trips to the pharmacy, massage therapy, counseling, ER visits, and many more visits to doctors…I was tired of it! I was a fixture in the waiting rooms. I began to accept that "this is just my lot." Some days I would tell God, "If I have to go through this, then please use it for your glory."

When I had the energy, I sowed encouragement to others in the waiting rooms and felt a bit of use to God. I had completely lost my sense of purpose in the big picture of God's plan. For years I told God, "If I have to be sick, if you choose not to heal me, then I'm okay with that." However, there was a warrior within me that kept saying, "No, this is not the way it is supposed to be!" Ultimately, I turned my prayer and supplication back to the Lord and humbly said, "Your will not mine, Lord," even if I didn't understand it.

Then I had the wake-up call. I was in for my full annual doctor visit and the scale tipped 299.9 pounds. I couldn't believe my eyes. Shame and embarrassment filled my being. So much so that I could barely look the nurse in the eye. I heard the whisper, "It's inevitable, you'll never lose weight. You will always be this way." I wanted to cry but had become a master at stuffing my feelings, so I swallowed them instead. It was clear this was not the whisper of God, but I felt powerless. My voice had escaped me.

We proceeded with the appointment and as I began to fill out the usual family medical history, the Holy Spirit said, "Don't fill it out the same way you always have." I was perplexed at His instructions. I read the questions and was prepared to answer them like any other time, but Holy Spirit said, "You are *not* your grandmother! You are living like you are and taking on her health issues. Your illness and genetics have become your identity. You have an illness mentality. You are *not* your grandmother. You shall live and not die!"

He was right. I had taken on the family culture and mindset. I accepted that I would be overweight and suffer with depression, anxiety, and nerve issues just like my grandmother—living in lack and bound to prescription medications the rest of my life. A vision of her flashed before me. She was a jovial soul, but she was overweight and sickly the majority of her life. She had already passed away, but I was keeping her alive with my mindset and lifestyle. I was carrying on the family cycle of the illness mentality and passing this generational thinking down to my children. I was buying into the lie of what the enemy and the world said was normal for aging, generational mindsets, and family medical issues. It had to stop!

I left the doctor's office that day with a tenacity about what the Holy Spirit had told me. I now saw that I had an upper hand on the enemy and God was giving me the opportunity to do something about it. My destiny this side of heaven weighed in the balance. I had a new reason to live and fight. I was fighting not only for myself; now I was fighting for my kids and the family generations to come!

Do not believe that you have to live out the medical, mental, or behavioral conditions of your ancestors. We have the ability to break the cycle, freeing us from the past. An illness mentality is not God's mentality.

Freedom Key

Choose to stop the generational cycle! See and believe in your own whole, divine, and unique design that was created by God.

Chapter 2
Displaying His Glory

I Am an Artist

> [12]Truly, truly, I say to you, he who believes in Me, the works that I do, he will do also; and greater works than these he will do; because I go to the Father. [13] Whatever you ask in My name, that will I do, so that the Father may be glorified in the Son. [14] If you ask Me anything in My name, I will do it. [15] If you love me, keep my commands. [16] I will ask the Father, and He will give you another Helper, that He may be with you forever; [17] that is the Spirit of truth, whom the world cannot receive, because it does not see Him or know Him, but you know Him because He abides with you and will be in you. [18] I will not leave you as orphans; I will come to you. [19] After a little while the world will no longer see Me, but you will see Me; because I live, you will live also. [20] In that day you will know that I am in My Father, and you in Me, and I in you. [21] He who has My commandments and keeps them is the one who loves Me; and he who loves Me will be loved by My Father, and I will love him and will disclose Myself to him.
>
> —John 14:12-21, NASB

Jesus told His disciples that when He is no longer with them in the flesh, He will remain with them. How confused the disciples must have been when Jesus spoke these words to them. He said this to prepare His disciples for the promise of the Holy Spirit. I can just imagine the doubt and questions that rose in their minds as they reflected on the memories they had made. He gave His word that He would not leave them as orphans; they would have a place and identity with and in Him. They would understand this eventually and had to trust in Him.

It is through the Holy Spirit that we come into relationship with Jesus, who restores us to the Father. It is by the leading and teaching of the Holy Spirit that we discover, cultivate, and grow as we yield to Him. Our callings and gifts should not define us but instead be a vehicle to release and display the Living God within us. This is key to understanding our identity and roles in the Kingdom of God.

I Want to Be an Artist!
Worldly Titles vs True Identity

To have a title is to feel important and accomplished; but to have the Giver of your life personally tell you who you are is so much more fulfilling. It changes everything.

"I want to be an artist!" The words rolled off my tongue, but doubt followed. "Am I even an artist?" I was looking for someone to settle this question once and for all and confirm my desire. For decades I felt unqualified as an artist because I didn't have the piece of paper—a diploma—saying I *was* an artist. Although something deep within me said I was an artist, the lack of a degree loomed over me.

Who am I? The better question to ask would be "God, who do You say I am?" but that is usually not our first question in the pursuit of identity. I was in such a dark and sad place of depression, oppressed with the mentality and spirit of infirmity. I began to ask, "God, why am I even here?" The question of "Who am I?" can send us on a search of discovery or cast us down to the pits of comparison. We often identify who we are by what we do or with whom we associate. It is awesome to think that the one who always comes in last, who is picked on and belittled, is the center of God's attention. Psalm 8:4 asks, "Who are we that HE is mindful of us?" Every day as we look in the mirror is a reminder of who we are: God's beloved children. But I didn't always see that.

This reaches far beyond titles and degrees. You may be carrying a family name, business, or trade that was passed down to you. Whatever the case, you have to find your own identity. It very well may be that you are a carpenter like your father, a nurse like your mother, or a seamstress like your grandmother; and that is fine as long as that is where God has led you. I could have taken on my family's restaurant business or become a lawyer like my dad, but that was not my passion. It wasn't what I was created to do. I'm thankful for those family businesses. They instilled a good work ethic in us, provided for us, and taught us valuable trades and life lessons.

Titles bring worldly validation and credibility but differ from your true identity and purpose in life. When I gave myself permission to be an artist, the ideal of a title grew dim. I came to understand that I was not just an earthly daughter but also a daughter of the King, with whom I was seated in heavenly places! (Ephesians 2:6) My true identity grew as I engaged with the Lord in co-creating at my easel. It was my spiritual glory spout, my green pasture, my most intimate and empowering secret place!

I grew in confidence and my toxic self-talk ceased. My whole perspective and the purpose of my gifts changed the day I realized that the reason I paint, the reason I do anything, is to display His glory! Our God-given talents are gifts, and they are responsibilities. It is called a gift for a reason. It is first for us and then for the world. Our gifts are given so that we can carry out assignments to benefit the Kingdom of God. What a privilege we have in being a part of bringing about the great big plan of God!

Why do we think we need permission? Where has that belief seed come from? It is a learned way of thinking passed down from generation to generation. Perhaps, it is something you heard from society time and time again. The book of James talks about the power of words and likens them to a ship under the control of the pilot setting a course, as well as having the ability to set fire.

> The tongue is a small part of the body, but it makes great boasts. Consider what a great forest is set on fire by a small spark. The tongue also is a fire, a world of evil among the parts of the body. It corrupts the whole body, sets the whole course of one's life on fire, and is itself on fire by hell.
>
> —James 3:5-6, NIV

I see this applying to good or evil. If words can rip us to shreds, then just think what they can do when used for good. Partner your motive with the living and active word of God and you will see miracles happen. I want to see the Holy Spirit use our words to set souls on fire for God, instead of destroying others. We allow others to speak into our lives because we are often seeking man's approval; this is usually the case when we are not secure in our identity in Christ. We let others steer our thoughts about ourselves, creating beliefs from their seeds.

Words are powerful and can turn a ship away from, or into, a storm. We have to steer our path away from our own self-sabotaging beliefs, and the toxic words of others, to align with where God desires us to be. By continually practicing this, we position ourselves for freedom and can walk in victory over the words of—and the need for approval from—others.

Are there false beliefs that need to be dismantled from your life that relate to your identity or gifting? Follow the exercise below to replace those false belief seeds with truth statements.

> *For He raised us from the dead along with Christ and seated us with him in the heavenly realms because we are united with Christ Jesus.*
>
> —Ephesians 2:6, NLT

Dismantling False Thinking

Validation Moment

One of the most profound moments of my life was when I heard the Lord call me His daughter and confirm in me that I was an artist and His minister. I want to help you experience the same thing. It starts with our acknowledging that He is our Heavenly Father who created us uniquely for His pleasure and purposes. Identity is a free gift in Him; and we must receive it and believe it.

Let me help dismantle and destroy the lies that you are unqualified, unworthy, or unknown just because you do not have the college degree, official title, or approval from man. God gives you permission and will guide you on your journey. He validates you!

Fill in the blank with a new declaration: I am a daughter/son of God and He created me to be a/an _____ _____. (This can be a title related to your gifts and talents, or even something that speaks to your natural personality, such as a singer, teacher, dancer, builder, writer, chef, nurse, etc.)

The reason I know this is because _____
_____
_____.

Examples include:

- I love bringing joy to people with music
- I love leading others in book studies
- I love hosting people at my home.
- I love cooking and creating new dishes and serving others.
- I love working with wood and seeing things built from scratch.

A great way to check your gift identity against the heart of God is to look at the fruit of the Spirit. I believe that when we use our gifts for God it creates and exercises the fruit of the Spirit in our lives. When we operate in our identity, gifts, and callings, then we feel fulfillment and joy.

THE FRUIT OF THE SPIRIT

Love, joy, peace, patience, kindness, goodness, faithfulness, gentleness, and self-control.
—Galatians 5:22-23, NIV

Does this reality ignite something within you? If yes, explain how your new declaration gives you vision, hope, and life. Expand on your previous answer in more detail.
_____
_____
_____

Re-write your gift identity story. Seal this new and true belief by re-writing your story and creating an "I am" declaration that you read and refer to regularly. Include your name, Son or Daughter of the Most-High God, your God-given gift, talent, or passion, and the purpose for which you will use it. Locate a scripture that aligns with your purpose or passion, and also list any life verses that speak to your identity in Christ. You can find a free PDF download of *The Art of Freedom* 'I am' identity statements at www.theartoffreedombook.com.

We need to take responsibility for our dreams and passions, they simply will not come about on their own. You do not need the title to give you permission to chase and embrace them. Stop watering the false belief seeds. Align your thoughts and dreams with Him, and He will position you for the opportunities to bring your identity and passions to life for His purposes and His glory. Remember, we do this so we can display His glory and be partakers in the kingdom.

Freedom Key

Steer your words in the way of truth and life to dismantle false beliefs. God gives you permission to use the gifts He has placed within you and validates you to fulfill the call He has placed on your life. Continue to declare this throughout your life.

Chapter 3
The Night the Veil Lifted

I Went from Just Believing to Seeing!

Is freedom a state of mind? Is it possible that we keep ourselves imprisoned in our minds by the way we think? How is it that we can be so blind with eyes wide open? Could it be that someone or some way of thinking has kept our mind and eyes veiled from the fullness of truth? Maybe no one has proposed that you think or see in a different way.

"It's mind over matter," I was told growing up. I've often wondered if this were true. This mind-over-matter concept challenged everything within me because my "reality" was telling me something different. When I looked in the mirror, I saw a weak and flawed physical appearance complicated by physical pain and an unrestored heart. Not to mention that I was falling short intellectually, according to the standards. Was this God's best for me—a life of pain, lack, and low self-esteem? I didn't feel that "I had made my bed and now I was sleeping in it." I just felt like something was missing, almost like it was being kept from me. I saw external realities instead of the greater reality waiting for me, a supernatural God reality. It took partnership with God to bring it to pass.

THE ART OF FREEDOM

I read the stories of Jesus telling people to pick up their mat and walk but I never paid much attention to it. I missed the full revelation of these biblical encounters. We usually focus on the healing, not the process. We want the miracle, the shock factor. We often miss the instructions He gave to the one being healed. Three things were required in this: faith, agreement, and obedience in action. I missed this practice of Jesus until I had a dramatic encounter with God that was accompanied by an instruction. He proposed His way of thinking and His perspective. He had been waiting for me to surrender to Him to awaken my soul to this new reality and finish His work in me. I believe without a shadow of a doubt that the prayers of people in my life brought me to this point.

> In every prayer for all of you, I always pray with joy, because of your partnership in the gospel from the first day until now, being confident of this, that He who began a good work in you will continue to perfect it until the day of Christ Jesus.
>
> —Philippians 1:6, NLT

The problem with the mind-over-matter theory is that it discounts the need for the Spirit's involvement; and we continue to believe that we can do this alone. But the truth is that we cannot do it for long apart from the Spirit of God. What we start in the soul and in the flesh, we must maintain in the soul and flesh. Before long, the method of a "soul or flesh" start will only exhaust us.

My dramatic encounter included the Father, Son, and the Holy Spirit separately yet all in one. They flooded my heart, awakened my soul, and opened my eyes once and for all. It was an unveiling. It was my pool of Bethesda moment! Dare I say that I had a born-again experience? My second awakening came eighteen years after I intentionally gave my heart to Jesus.

THE NIGHT THE VEIL LIFTED

It was the night of March 12, 2016. My husband and I were attending The Crabb Family concert at Free Chapel Church in Spartanburg, South Carolina. I had faithfully followed this family of singers and their individual ministries for more than ten years. Their music was grounded in scriptural truth, always speaking to the heart and issues of today, and timeless in its message and impact. I particularly resonated with the message of hope from Jason, the lead singer. God used his music to help me through times of pain and depression. In this dark time of my life I forced myself to replace the thoughts of wanting to leave this earth with a song of hope sung by this group. I would fall asleep at night with tears drenching my pillow while I listened to Jason sing "Daystar" or "I'd Rather Have Jesus." On other days I claimed the powerful message of their hit "Through the Fire." The songs were like balm to my wounded and weary soul. The Holy Spirit took their musical gifts that night and caused hearts to respond. My life changed that night. I was marked by something I will never forget.

It was the last night of their tour and they were raring to go, but the crowd was dead.

The family came out, warmed up the crowd, and about thirty minutes into the concert Jason told the audience, "This is our last night and we're gonna give you all we've got." I was hungry for the Spirit to move; but the lack of energy in the audience was stifling it. I was tired, had been through the wringer with my health, and was ready for an awesome and powerful move of God. I was in a fight for my life and I went there to encounter His presence! I was there in expectation, ready to reach for the hem of Jesus's garment.

Pure excitement lit my soul. They sang one of their classics that pierced my heart, and tears began to flow. Then Jason changed the tune—literally. He began to sing, "Holy Spirit, You Are Welcome Here." The Holy Spirit moved and suddenly

I felt I had been pushed out of my chair, and found myself on my knees at the altar. It was an involuntary response. I was on my knees less than a minute when Aaron, Jason's brother, came over, laid a hand on my head, and prayed over me. I could not hear what he was saying because of the music. I just felt this incredible weight of God's presence come over me. I felt compassion from Aaron. I knew it was a direct line of compassion from Christ. All I could do was weep before my Lord. I was so tired. The burden was heavy. The fight had really worn me down. I was living in a cycle of defeat and didn't know how to stop it.

I had become the woman in the crowd grasping for the hem of Jesus's garment, persistent and hungry for healing. In Mark 5, the woman with the issue of the blood had suffered many things from many physicians. She spent all she had and was not any better, but instead grew worse (Mark 5:25-34, NKJV). This was my story, too. I was ready to give up on life all together.

After Aaron finished praying for me, I felt a slight breeze and something touched me ever so lightly on my forehead. Down I went like a wooden beam. I thought it was a person, but the touch didn't feel human. After a few minutes I heard a whisper that said, "Get up." I responded, "I don't want to get up." Again, the voice said "Get up"; but the tone was louder and firmer. I did not want to get up. One last time I said, "I give up. I don't want to get up. Lord, please help me. I can't do this anymore. I'm tired of fighting this illness. I'm tired of living this life." I argued with God like a little child unwilling to obey.

What I said next is what I believe changed the game. I said, "Lord, I'm begging you, please help me and heal me or take me home." I got real with God; it was not well with my soul and it was out. I said it! I basically told God that dying would be okay. I am so thankful that was not His choice and that He chose to heal me and help me get up instead.

Then He spoke: "Daughter, don't give up. I've got you. You can't give up; I have work for you to do. Daughter, you must get up!" I saw an arm reach down to me with a hand extended in the spirit. It was clearly an invitation to help me up. I reached past His hem and grabbed hold of His hand. When I grabbed the hand in the vision, I saw my spirit rise but I was physically still on the ground.

Immediately following that vision, I felt a rumbling that started inside my gut. I was trembling but in no pain and I was not afraid. The rumbling in my gut intensified, like a jack hammer. I heard the Lord tell me He was doing surgery in the deepest part of me. The rumbling came from a place where two lives had been stolen from me—my womb—and where I desperately needed healing in spirit, soul, and body. It was the innermost part of me, where the Holy Spirit dwells and where life is born. He was cleaning house and tilling the ground so new life could fill it and soon out of my belly rivers of living water would flow (John 7:38, NKJV).

This was the first time I had heard Him call me "daughter" and in some way my heart was sealed in a new identity! Not only did He seal it in my heart, it also resonated in my mind and I agreed. From that moment on I truly saw myself as His daughter.

I opened my eyes and realized my head was in a woman's lap. She was stroking my hair and praying over me. I looked up at her and she smiled with kind eyes and helped me sit up. When I sat up, I looked around, still with tears in my eyes, and what I saw blew my mind and gripped my heart at the same time. In a matter of minutes, I literally went from just believing to seeing!

The altar was packed! People were everywhere. I thought, what happened? Something was very different. I was seeing differently, like when you wash the dirt and bugs off your windshield. Everything was crystal clear. I immediately had complete clarity in the spirit and peace in my mind and body!

I heard weeping and cries of desperation. In the spirit I saw broken hearts laid on the altar floor. I felt their disappointments, their sorrow, their questions. I saw the pain and suffering in their hearts. I was feeling their hearts and what the heart of God was feeling as well. I felt it all! Members of the Crabb family came down from the stage and went from person to person, praying. My weeping for myself turned to weeping for others.

I just sat there and bawled my eyes out as I watched people cry and pour out their hearts before the Lord. Then Kelly, one of the family singers, came by and cradled my face in her hands. She looked right at me and said, "Jesus loves you!" I responded with sincerity, "Thank you." I returned to my seat and the Crabb family broke for intermission. I could have gone home right then; but it was one of those nights I didn't want to end. I'm so thankful that Jason shifted the atmosphere that night. It was an appointed time for me in my life, a marker moment, and Love had broken through!

What Have You Done?

"I got closer to the Light so I'm much brighter now."

The day after the concert I woke up with my new eyes and healed mind. My eyes still saw clearly, and my mind was completely unveiled. I felt like a new woman. I had suffered with memory fog and confusion from multiple prescription medications. It was gone, completely gone! I felt empowered from that day on to begin eliminating the rest of my prescriptions. The voice that Satan once had silenced had re-emerged. God had given me courage, confidence, and trust; and I was ready to move forward by His leading. I had found my voice in the valley of desolation, desperation, and isolation. All the years of fear, anxiety, poor self-worth, and pain melted away at the sound of His voice. His words lingered and mingled with my spirit. I arose, picked up my mat, and walked. I wasn't going to stuff my feelings any longer, nor discount my validity and worth, allowing Satan or man to silence my voice. I now had a voice of determination, victory, and love! My very identity and authority in Christ were awakened like never before!

Since that night my eyes have physically become clearer and brighter in color. People began asking "What have you done?" I told them, "I got closer to the Light so I'm much brighter now." They say that I look radiant and vibrant, and that they see joy, power, peace, and confidence in me. My only explanation is Him! This started my season of seeing clearer visions and having vivid dreams again, which continue today.

The following weeks proved that my God encounter and spiritual renovation was real. My life would never be the same. I became more sensitive to spiritual things in the atmosphere for the purpose of intercession. My gift of discernment had gotten a major upgrade. The enemy had been exposed and he had picked the wrong girl to mess with for all those years!

The daughter who sought to touch His hem in Mark 5 had great faith, but she put action behind it and reached out. I love that Jesus called her daughter, just like he did me that night. His power healed her body. Christ addressed the condition of her heart and spoke to her very identity in a whole-person encounter—spirit, soul, and body—that brought restoration.

Desiring to reach only the hem of His garment cannot be enough for healing and sustained freedom. We need to be a people of hunger and persistence as we seek the LORD, pressing past the hem with faith, taking hold of the Promiser. I am confident that when we do this, we will experience whole-person restoration and transformation.

Jesus said, "If you can believe, all things are possible to him (or her) who believes" (Mark 9:23, NKJV).

THE ART OF FREEDOM

Freedom Key

Our faith pleases God. By faith and action, we are healed through God's grace. Faith, agreement with God, hunger, persistence, and obedience in action are powerful components to live a healed, whole, and free life. Don't let the enemy steal your authority, voice, or position in Christ.

Chapter 4
I'm Healing You

"But Seek First..."

It was the day after Easter and my spirit was still on a high from the day before as we celebrated the Resurrection of Christ. This Easter was different. There was an excitement in my spirit I had not had in a very long time. I knew Jesus was alive and my spirit was on fire since my encounter sixteen days earlier. For months, the Holy Spirit had been speaking to me first thing in the morning as I lingered between sleep and waking. I opened my eyes after a good night's sleep, breathing in forced air through my c-pap machine, and I heard, "I'm healing you." I froze, staring up at the ceiling, and waited. I heard it again, "I'm healing you."

It was a voice that filled the room. I had never heard it like this before. If the words had been physical matter, they would have been hanging right in front of me in the atmosphere. I was caught off guard. After a short pause He repeated himself. I heard it again but with more firmness and authority: "I'M HEALING YOU!" I ripped off my c-pap mask, sat up, and whipped around to the edge of the bed. I gasped and with a quiver in my voice said, "You're healing me?" He responded, "Yes, you have prayed for me to heal you for years." Then I said, "I know I did but..." and He finished my statement, "but you weren't sure when." I said, "Yes." The thought "stop doubting" came to mind. I immediately began to repent and asked the Lord for forgiveness for any unbelief. I had always believed in faith, but my heart had become weary in the waiting. I became overwhelmed with tears and laid back down and lifted my arms towards the ceiling thanking Him as I wept uncontrollably. I was praising and thanking Him then my insides started to convulse. I looked down and literally saw them moving up, down, and around. It was like somebody was in there with a jack hammer, just like the night at the concert. Then the power and fire of God radiated to my arms and legs. I was trembling from the power of God and speaking in tongues rapidly. I began to feel a sensation in my legs with a shifting of temperatures. It was cool then warm and cool again. I could feel the heaviness and pain leaving my legs. After forty minutes the sensations and waves of trembling began to subside. I managed to reach over to my nightstand and called my husband so I could have some sort of witness. Through tears I told Will, "He said He is healing me, He's healing me!" He rejoiced and praised God with me. He responded, "Praise God" with an emotional quiver in his voice.

    I hung up the phone and wept at how good and loving my LIVING GOD was. I felt like His eyes were on me and only me at that moment. As I lay there, decades of physical, mental, and emotional hell flashed through my mind, and now it was completely gone! I had lived in a prison in my mind and body for so long I began to wonder, "How do I even begin to walk in this new normal?" I recalled all the times it was tough and almost unbearable, but He showed me how He was there. Even in my darkest, most painful moments, He was there.

    I believe healing begins in the heart and mind first then it will eventually manifest itself in the physical body. It's necessary to restore the heart and act upon forgiveness to others and ourselves. This does not negate the power of God. He can and will miraculously heal in a moment's time. With God being sovereign, He will do what is according to His divine will and nature; but He, too, has to abide by the spiritual and physical laws He has put into place. As our sovereign Judge, He has the final say, but we are able to approach him confidently in humility, repent, and receive forgiveness, which results in us being restored. We can take back territory and remove legal right from the enemy in the courts of Heaven.

I explain this more in chapter six "The Art of Restoring the Heart." Robert Henderson is an authority on this topic and teaches about the courts of Heaven according to the scriptures in his book *Operating in the Courts of Heaven.* From what I have seen, read, and personally experienced, I believe healing comes down to four reasons. One, Jesus healed people out of God's grace and His compassion. Two, Jesus healed to create signs and wonders by performing miracles for testimony to unbelievers. Three, Jesus healed when He saw great faith and sins were forgiven. And, four, Jesus healed when He knew that the recipient of the healing would always give God the glory and point people to Jesus. It is important to understand that we must keep a humble spirit before the LORD and keep a repentant heart daily, putting action to our faith and living with expectation. Repentance always unlocks healing but ultimately mercy and compassion are at the heart of healing and it is ALWAYS God's will to heal.

My Matthew 6:33 Plan
Seek First

Following my healing encounter, the Lord spoke to me one day saying that I needed to continue to "seek Him first in all things." I thought I was putting Him first in my life by going to church and raising my children to love and serve Him, but there were areas in my heart I still was not surrendering to Him. I became intentional and vigilant in my time with Him, putting into place my Matthew 6:33 plan. I had to put forth effort and seek out first what I needed to do to protect my healing and walk in the fullness of all He had for me. This was just the beginning.

> *But seek first His kingdom and His righteousness, and all these things will be added to you.*
> —Matthew 6:33, NASB

I scheduled time with Him first thing in the morning, reading and meditating on the Truth of His Word, praying and listening for his voice, lingering. I began expecting Him to speak. I maintained an attitude of prayer and fellowship throughout my days. I replaced TV shows with biblical teaching videos and talk radio with faith-building podcasts. I had an insatiable hunger for Him and His word. It was no longer a religious chore, instead it became my desire. I had tasted and seen that He is good! The fire of God had set itself in my soul and was burning brighter than ever before. I refused to be a playground for the enemy any longer. He had laughed at me and made a joke of me long enough.

As old thought patterns tried to return, or the whisper of the enemy came, I would speak in faith with the written word of God and admonish the enemy. I had to take destructive thoughts captive to allow the Holy Spirit to renew my mind.

Shortly after my healing encounter, I sealed this event with water baptism at a women's conference called "Stronger," hosted by Kathy Crabb Hannah. Before the conference, I knew that they were going to have a baptism service in the hotel pool, but I had not planned on participating. I had been baptized before, but the Holy Spirit moved on me in a strong and undeniable way the day of the baptisms. That afternoon I knew I was going to get baptized again as I listened to the Isaacs sing "Waiting in the Water." I was determined to bury all those years of illness and everything that went with it. More than two hundred people were in the pool area that night. We sang and worshiped the Lord; I watched and waited my turn. The scene resembled the slow "Just as I am" Billy Graham Crusade walk, with people shuffling closer to the pool as the waters were being stirred like the waters at the pool of Bethesda.

My turn came and I was both excited and nervous. I entered the pool and the warm water greeted my newly healed body. I was brimming with excitement and anticipation but also with righteous determination. I was about to put Satan under my feet for good! Two ladies greeted me and asked why I was getting baptized. I responded, "I am burying ten-plus years of illness in this water and coming up new because the Lord has healed me! New spirit, new mind, new body." They rejoiced with me, prayed over me, and plunged me into the water. I came up rejoicing with a trembling in my gut again, just like the morning He spoke to me in my bedroom and the night at the concert. I was overcome with tears of joy. It was a beautiful event to experience and see all those women renewing their faith and expressing their desire to start anew.

By seeking Him and His righteousness first, we create a fellowship with the Holy Spirit that will sustain us. Proverbs 4:20-23 became a life verse for me: "My son, give attention to my words; Incline your ear to my sayings. Do not let them depart from your eyes; Keep them in the midst of your heart; For they are life to those who find them, And health to all their flesh. Keep your heart with all diligence; For out of it spring the issues of life." (NKJV)

There are only two options: seek Him or not. Either way we will reap the results. The freedom found in His words far outweighs the freedom the world offers. His freedom is for our benefit and for His glory.

THE ART OF FREEDOM

Freedom Key

Surrender and seek first His kingdom and His righteousness. Live a humble and repentant lifestyle before the LORD. Release offense and forgive others quickly!

Chapter 5
Vision Births Hope

From Invitation to Participation

There is something powerful about vision; and if we choose to take hold of it, the outcome could be completely life changing! As a visual artist I am impacted by what I see. We need a belief system and a filter because what we believe we will become. Vision can birth hope. Vision shows us who we are, where we are headed, and who we could become. Before the foundations of the earth were laid and before you were physically created, you were part of God's vision and divine design. He created you for good and not for destruction. Your destiny is for greatness and not defeat, to live fully alive now and eternally with Him.

In one of the darkest and loneliest times of my life I was given a vision. I was deeply oppressed and depressed. I had lost all purpose in life. I felt worthless, misplaced from society, and simply a failure as a wife and mother. God knew exactly where I was and where I was headed if I didn't make a change. On one of the many isolated days, I was at home, a prisoner in my mind. It was on this day that the LORD gave me a vision and a promise. It took me by surprise because my present circumstances were opposite of the vision and promise. I wrote the vision down and said to Him, "Really God, how is that going to happen when I am obviously not fit to do that in my condition. Who am I?" He responded, "Your condition is not who you are; you are I AM STRONG!" The words "I am, I AM STRONG" echoed in my head. Eventually my spirit began to identify with that. The promise and truth lined up with a popular scripture: "I can do all things through Christ who strengthens me" (Philippians 4:13, NKJV). I immediately knew the LORD was speaking to my identity and my destiny. The word and vision from the LORD were an invitation to a greater identity and way of thinking and living. Now it was my turn to receive it and believe it through faith. It took one vision, one spoken word, and one choice to change my outcome. I took that vision and that moment of divine encounter, began to believe it, and refused to give up. I insisted on overcoming, so I put in place the practice of P.U.S.H. (Persevere Until Something Happens); then I persevered some more. I felt a power and grit rise up within me that propelled me forward. It was something no person could have done for me. It was God and God alone! I had waited eight years for His promises and my prayers to come to pass. I felt I had been given a gift of renewed strength to persevere. But the freedom and healing would not come without a fight!

When we take hold of the visions and dreams God gives us, it can carry us through the darkest and most trying times of life; and I believe that vision births hope!

Two Dreams, Two Outcomes
Which One Will You Choose?

> *Let not mercy and truth forsake you; Bind them around your neck, write them on your heart, and so find favor and high esteem in the sight of God and man.*
> —Proverbs 3:3-4 NKJV

Genesis chapter 40 tells a story of two people with two different outcomes. Joseph was accused of something he did not do and, when Pharaoh found out, he was placed in prison. Because Joseph was innocent the LORD was with him, showed him mercy, and gave him favor in the sight of the prison keeper. Because the LORD was with him, whatever he did, the LORD made it prosper (Genesis 39:21,23 NKJV).

While Joseph was in the prison, two of Pharaoh's officers were placed there with him and Joseph was charged to serve them. One was Pharaoh's cupbearer, the other his chief baker. After they had been in custody for some time, both of Pharaoh's officers had a dream the same night. When Joseph arrived the next morning, he saw that they were depressed. He asked them, "Why do you look so sad today?" They responded, "We both had dreams, but there is no one to interpret them for us."

Joseph responded, "Do not interpretations belong to God? Tell them to me, please." Right here I want to point out Joseph's acknowledgement of God and his own confidence to hear God. He knew his identity and he knew God. The story continues and the chief cupbearer tells Joseph about his dream, saying: "In my dream, I saw a vine in front of me and on the vine were three branches. As soon as it budded, it blossomed, and its clusters ripened into grapes. Pharaoh's cup was in my hand,

and I took the grapes, and squeezed them into Pharaoh's cup, and put the cup in his hand." (NIV)

"This is what the dream means," Joseph replied. "The three branches are three days. Within three days, Pharaoh will lift up your head and restore you to your position and you will put his cup into his hand just as you did when you were his cupbearer." When the chief baker heard the cupbearer's favorable interpretation of his dream, he said to Joseph, "I too had a dream: On my head were three baskets of bread. In the top basket were all kinds of baked goods for Pharaoh but the birds were eating them out of the basket on my head." (NIV)

Joseph replied, "This is what it means. The three baskets are three days. Within three days Pharaoh will lift off your head and impale your body on a pole, and the birds will eat away at your flesh." Now it came to pass on the third day, which was Pharaoh's birthday, that he made a feast for all his servants; and he lifted up the head of the chief butler and of the chief baker among his servants. Then he restored the chief butler to his butlership again, and he placed the cup in Pharaoh's hand. But he hanged the chief baker, just as Joseph had interpreted to them (Genesis 40, NKJV).

One of the dreams was of physical life and restoration, the other was a physical and possibly a spiritual death. Both parties were imprisoned, both were given dreams but with two different outcomes. Because of their offense to the King of Egypt they were rightfully in prison; but why after serving their sentence was their destiny different? Could the baker have done something different after receiving the interpretation of his dream to change the course of his life? I'd like to believe the answer is yes. Did he just accept this as his lot in life? Perhaps he did not bother to believe for a better life or outcome.

I'd like to think that God gave the dream to the baker for him to at least examine his ways and possibly change, at least have a change of heart, regardless of the outcome. This could have been his wake-up call! I believe both dreams were initiated by God even though they had opposite outcomes. This reflects God's design of divine will and permissive will. He gives us the opportunity to choose and to change.

I like to think of dreams and visions as God's way of showing us movie trailers of things concerning our life and the lives of others. Picture it: you're sitting in the comfort of your own home, you have a bowl of fresh popcorn in your lap, you settle in to watch your movie, and the previews begin to play. A clip flashes on the screen, then an announcer's voice says, "Coming soon to a life near you!" The film is starring you, others you know, and some you may not know. You are now a lead actor or actress in God's next blockbuster film. We know God's plan is not a Hollywood movie; but He is the most brilliant director and producer, so I tend to take notice when He shares clips from His films with me. Dreams and visions from God are visual inspirations from Him and a way that He communicates with us metaphorically in hopes of engaging our spirits and affecting our hearts. Dreams and visions that carry a prophetic nature have to align with His word and the intent of His heart. His heart is that you should have life and have it abundantly, and that none should perish. He is completely for you and not against you. This is the divine will of God: for you to live all your days with your heart devoted to Him and His purposes for His glory. We must choose to believe this, receive it, and act on it. By doing this, we are partnering with the Holy Spirit for the purposes of God and for our good. Your next vision or dream could be a personal invitation from God to engage in conversation with Him and participate in His plan by seeking greater understanding and insight.

My French Fry Vision

"The Fat Is Killing You!"

One morning as I turned my thoughts to the Lord, I had a vision of a crisp golden crinkle-cut french fry. Yep, a french fry. It was hanging right in front of me; and I heard the Holy Spirit say, "Stop eating that junk. The fat is killing you!"

It's a funny story but it was a very serious moment because He was right! All my life I had been in bondage to food. I was now at 299.9 pounds and the fat *was* killing me! It wasn't only french fries. I had a terrible relationship with food, and it showed! More importantly, I had a poor relationship with myself, and food was simply an avenue of comfort to numb my fear and pain.

This vision wasn't God condemning me. He was giving me an opportunity to make a change. He was using this vision as a way to get to the root of the problem. His desire was for me to be well, healthy, and whole, as it is for you!

I could have ignored it and kept on living my life the way I wanted to, but I couldn't. You just can't ignore stuff like that! If I had ignored it, I might not have lived to write this book.

I sought the Lord and began to ask Him to give me strength in these areas of weakness. Then the Holy Spirit took away my cravings for unhealthy food and replaced them with a desire to eat well and to help my family and others do the same. More importantly, He gave me a craving for His word and His ways.

As I yielded and submitted my will and desires to the Holy Spirit, the fruit of the Spirit, self-control began to be produced in my life. The power of the Holy Spirit began helping me to stop overeating and to cut my portion sizes in half. No longer did I want food to fill me. I wanted all He had for me; His presence and the living word were satisfying my soul and my stomach.

It was evidence of His governing presence in my life as I continued to apply the fruit of self-control, accompanied by

His wisdom, to do what was right and not justify my desires for what was not best. We can trust that God's way, through the Holy Spirit, will always lead us into truth, life, purity, and wholeness.

This was the beginning of my physical healing. My restored heart was singing, my soul was thriving, and now my body was displaying the fruit from within.

Visions and dreams can propose life or death, but the intended purpose is to birth hope. God's motive is always to give hope and birth life.

Freedom Key

Watch and listen for God-given inspirations, dreams, and visions. Document them in a journal and ask the Holy Spirit how to pray into them. Check them against scripture, record the scriptures that line up with the message. Hold onto the inspirations, dreams, and visions for hope!

Note: There are often levels of dreams and visions for the purpose of intercession. As you mature in the Lord and you begin to walk in a greater area of calling or authority, God may give you dreams and visions for greater intercession purposes. He may be calling you to pray for local or regional issues, nations, governments, justice issues, or certain groups of people. This is usually the calling and assignment of a "watchman." Not all intercessors are prophets, but you can be sure that 99.9% of the time prophets are intercessors. Two examples in the Bible are Jeremiah and Deborah. Both of them were intercessors and both were prophets. I found that the Lord developed my intercession calling long before my prophetic gift because of the person I needed to become in the secret place with Him. Be sure to pay attention to spiritual patterns developing or any dreams and visions that He gives specifically for you. Acquire a trustworthy dreams and visions resource for processing and looking up metaphoric information after seeking the Holy Spirit. I highly recommend *The Divinity Code* by Adam Thompson. I believe it is the most thorough and accurate resource available on this topic.

Reflect and Record in Your Journal

Do you see a pattern of an unhealthy relationship with vices in your life? Do you have an unhealthy relationship with food or some other vice to fill your voids, numb your pain, and free you from your fears? Take a few moments and reflect on this. Journal your thoughts and ask the Holy Spirit to reveal any other vices. Jesus wants to be the One to fill your every void and Holy Spirit is here to help you overcome and walk free!

Dream and Vision Activation

Ask the Lord to speak to you through dreams while your sleep or to make you more aware of visual images and impressions while you're awake. Ask Him to give you eyes to see, ears to hear, and a mind to know and understand.

Prayer empowerment

Heavenly Father, in the name of Jesus, I come to you in my weakness. Lord, you know my weaknesses and how I use food, drink, shopping, or other worldly thing to fill my void and comfort my heart. I repent for doing this and for not honoring and treating my body as the temple of the Living God. I ask you to forgive me. Please reveal the root of my unhealthy vice issue and tend to it in my heart. Holy Spirit, please help me surrender this to you and do what is right in your eyes, Lord. Show me who I am in you, as well as the healthy and whole plans that you have for me, so I can live in victory over this stronghold. I thank you for breaking this stronghold and replacing it with the stronghold of the Lord! Help me to yield to your work today and empower me to walk free from emotional bondage with eating or any other unhealthy habit. Thank you for setting me free. By faith I believe and receive my healing now in the name of Jesus. Amen.

PART TWO

The Art of Restoring the Heart: Humility, Surrender, and Forgiveness

Chapter 6
THE ART OF RESTORING THE HEART

You Were Made to Live Whole!

The spirit of a man will sustain him in sickness, but who can bear a broken spirit?
—Proverbs 18:14, NKJV

Have you ever felt heartsick? We all have. It is just part of life. Feeling is part of being alive. Most of us suck it up, stuff it down, or lash out. But not dealing with the root of the heart sickness creates a toxic terrain. Often, we use a vice of some sort to cope with our personal pain. For me that vice was food. It was a way to cover up and escape my hurting heart.

As I sit down to tackle probably the hardest part of this book, I hear the phrase "Just bleed, Dee, just bleed," derived from a quote by one my favorite writers, Ernest "Papa" Hemingway. He said, "There is nothing to writing. All you do is sit down at a typewriter and bleed." Hemingway was no stranger to physical and emotional pain. In some strange way, at the age of sixteen I resonated with this mysteriously gifted man and his struggle. I admired his multi-cultured and exotic lifestyle, and had big dreams of traveling internationally as a creative person. Both of our artistic hearts were susceptible to pain, defeat, and disappointment.

In 1988 my parents and I took a spring break trip to Key West. I loved the Keys for their tropical atmosphere; and Key West particularly had a quaintness with the colorful homes, palm-lined streets, and open-air restaurants and bars. It was different and exciting to this free-spirited teenager. It carried an "old beach" nostalgic feel that was different from the rest of the world.

While there, we toured the house where Hemingway lived and wrote for ten years. The grounds were lush with tropical vegetation and provided a home for up to fifty cats at a time. A large majority of the cats were six-toed. My parents thought I would get a kick out of that since I was born with six toes on my right foot. My pinkie toe was heart-shaped where two bones and two nails merged. At age twenty-two, I had the extra toe removed because it was painful. Periodically over the years my mom would bring up the six-toed cats and we would laugh about it.

Touring the Hemingway property was like stepping back in time and going around the world at the same time with the nostalgic décor and gardens. I could feel his soul there. I could sense it was a place of solace and struggle. It was an honor to walk the grounds and see his typewriter where he brilliantly bled. He had a way of taking his life experiences and transforming them into incredible novels.

I believe Hemingway suffered from an unrestored heart and generational issues that manifested in his life in different ways. He was diagnosed, and potentially misdiagnosed, with depression accompanied by alcoholism. Little did I know my unrestored heart would eventually manifest in self-sabotaging ways as well.

I identified with Hemingway's love of sun, water, salty air, and adventure, but did not realize that, like him, I was developing vices that stemmed from generational issues. His escape was often on the water for extended periods of time. I began to recognize a pattern of escape in my own life. Merriam-Webster describes *escapism* as a "habitual diversion of the mind to purely imaginative activity or entertainment as an escape from reality or routine." Like Hemingway, I was looking for a way to alleviate my malady. I wanted to live a transformed life but thought imagination and escape was the only way to do so; and therefore, I sought alternative and temporary remedies.

The quest to live out a dream propels some to pursue that vision with all their might. For others it remains a dream blocked by adversaries—both ourselves and Satan. The journey to escape a modern-day Egypt and to be all you were created to be truly is a quest to be transformed and free.

In the *Transformers* movies, we see this very scenario. It's much different from Hemingway's stories but also addresses identity, purpose, struggle, loss, defeat, victory, and the pursuit of freedom. Who wouldn't want to be a vehicle that could be transformed into something more beautiful, powerful, and designed to carry out a good purpose? That was my desire. The problem was that what I wanted and how I saw myself were total opposites. I saw myself as an old, worn-out, broken-down Volkswagen bug when I wanted the power and look of a shiny Camaro. My perspective and desire were based on the wrong things. I saw others as shiny Camaros. The lies of poor self-worth nearly paralyzed me to the point of giving up. Eventually this came to a screeching halt. I finally learned that I had the power within me, through Jesus and the Holy Spirit, to make that happen.

Those us of who have suffered from an untreated hurting heart, defeated mentality, or dark thinking can function in society quite well. We may even seem to be extroverts and the life of the party; but actually, we are quite the opposite. We hide behind the smile on our face. This became the story of my adult years. I was smiling on the outside but dying on the inside! Society has taught us to sweep it under the rug, look the other way, and especially don't burden others with our problems. We can be the life of the party, but we fall apart when we return to our own safe zone. We begin to examine and criticize ourselves and retreat into a place of self-doubt, self-rejection, and low self-worth. The end result is incredible and indescribable sadness and isolation: a tool of the enemy.

It is hard to understand how someone so loved and talented could have so much self-rejection, self-doubt, and low self-worth. Opinions of others cause us to have a distorted perception of ourselves. Our perception and reflection should be one with that of Christ. It comes down to understanding the love that God has for us and the love we have for ourselves.

What we are about to tackle in the pages to come will be both challenging and victorious. No victory comes without a battle. The important thing to remember is that the ultimate battle has been won by Jesus Christ on the cross.

One of the hardest things you can hear when you are suffering with a hurting heart is to "suck it up" or "it's all in your head." We have to allow Holy Spirit to renew our minds and retrain our brains, but first we have to heal our hearts.

The prophet Isaiah spoke on two particular occasions of One who would come and deal with us, tenderly restoring our hearts. That One is Jesus. "A bruised reed He will not break, and smoking flax He will not quench; He will bring forth justice for truth" (Isaiah 42:3, NKJV).

The reeds were used to make flutes and flax was used to make the wicks of oil lamps. This metaphor represents the condition of the hearts of people. A bruised reed could not produce the sound for which it was created; and a wick that was not trimmed would create smoke and dim the light from the lamp. The Amplified Bible describes the flax as a dimly burning wick, representing the downtrodden or dejected in heart.

Isaiah expands on the previous text with a prophecy about the coming of the Lord.

> [1]The Spirit of the Lord God is upon me,
> Because the Lord has anointed and commissioned me
> To bring good news to the humble and afflicted;
> He has sent me to bind up [the wounds of] the brokenhearted,
> To proclaim release [from confinement and condemnation] to the [physical and spiritual] captives
> And freedom to prisoners,
> [2]To proclaim the favorable year of the Lord,
> And the day of vengeance and retribution of our God,
> To comfort all who mourn,
> [3]To grant to those who mourn in Zion the following:
> To give them a turban instead of dust [on their heads, a sign of mourning],
> The oil of joy instead of mourning,
> The garment [expressive] of praise instead of a disheartened spirit.
> So, they will be called the trees of righteousness [strong and magnificent, distinguished for integrity, justice, and right standing with God],
> The planting of the Lord, that He may be glorified.
> [4]Then they will rebuild the ancient ruins,
> They will raise up and restore the former desolations;
> And they will renew the ruined cities,
> The desolations (deserted settlements) of many generations.
>
> —Isaiah 61:1-4, Amplified Bible

THE ART OF FREEDOM

I recognized that I was that bruised reed and dimly burning wick. I needed the oil of joy to rebuild the ruins of my heart. I was living with a broken spirit after decades of not recognizing how my heart was sabotaging me with emotions from traumatic events. If the purpose is for us to be a light in the world, then our heart must be like a well-tended lamp so we can light the way for others. Until we are filled and whole with the Living God, we will only struggle to keep our own light burning, without making a dent in the darkness.

As I thought about Hemingway and his struggles in life my heart broke for him. With his emotional and physical traumas in life he sank deeper and deeper into what they originally diagnosed as depression and possibly bipolar disorder.

We live much of our lives on an emotional rollercoaster, not knowing the root cause of depression or sadness, and we begin to accept it as a way of life. God gave us our ability to feel and respond emotionally, but we must learn to do this in a healthy way. God is faithful and all-knowing. Through prayer, the Holy Spirit can reveal to us what the root is so that we can put an axe to it and be healed and restored. His will is always to heal! He created us and no one knows us better. My Master Counselor is the Holy Spirit. When we walk in relationship with Him, He will reveal what needs to be healed at the appropriate time. The Lord will cause your dimly burning wick to blaze again and He promises to strengthen you through it all.

Hope deferred makes the heart sick, but a desire fulfilled is a tree of life.

—Proverbs 13:12, ESV

Freedom Key

When a past hurt is revealed, immediately take it to the Lord and ask Holy Spirit to come and minister to your heart. Listen to His promptings and respond accordingly. Trust that God knows what He is doing and be willing to wait on the Lord!

Reflect and Record in Your Journal

Have you had a dream or situation trigger an unpleasant memory or past hurt? If so, how did you deal with it in the moment? Did you respond in a healthy manner or did you react in a negative way, allowing it to dictate your emotions and actions? Do you feel like you remain a slave to your emotions? Ask the Holy Spirit to show you how to submit your hurts and emotions to the Lordship of Christ Jesus. Receive healing once and for all from the situation and yield to His healing hand. Record your results.

Prayer Empowerment

Heavenly Father, in the name of Jesus, I need you. I recognize that I am not living fully in the blessing that you died to give me. I repent for any unforgiveness or bitterness that I may be harboring in my heart, and I ask you to forgive me and to help me forgive myself and others who have hurt me. Holy Spirit, search my heart and show me the areas of my life and my heart that need to be healed and surrendered to Jesus. I ask that you gently tend to that area of my heart as I face some very deep and hurtful issues, and choose to cling to You and your promises. I am trusting you with my heart and choosing to agree with your Word. I receive your love and yield to your work. I thank you for loving me, forgiving me, and healing me. Amen.

Chapter 7
THE ART OF GENERATIONAL FREEDOM

It was for freedom that Christ set us free; therefore, keep standing firm and do not be subject again to a yoke of slavery.
—Galatians 5:1, NASB

While I understood Ernest Hemingway's pain, I saw the root of his "mental illness" for what it was. First, it was generationally rooted in spiritual strongholds. Seven suicides in the Hemingway family point to a generational curse. Transgressions, iniquities, and sin are a gateway to the soul and a way for generational strongholds to be erected that will remain unless someone breaks the cycle. Second, it was complicated by war trauma that affected the mind, accidents that caused brain trauma, and the physical lifestyle he chose as a heavy drinker. All of these accumulated and drove him to his death. It starts in the spirit, affects the mind, then manifests in the body. This cannot be ignored or denied. There was a curse and a pattern followed.

A generational illness or curse is a spiritual stronghold that is passed down from one generation to another. As you walk in Christ, it is possible to break these curses and stop the cycle in your life and in your children's lives. We are susceptible to spiritual, emotional, mental, and physical issues if the sin of our ancestors has not been addressed. We must give God permission to move on our behalf and remove the legal right Satan has taken and used to build a case against us, torment us, and cause us to suffer.

> Keeping mercy for thousands, forgiving iniquity and transgression and sin, and that will by no means clear the guilty; visiting (punishing) the iniquity of the fathers upon the children, and upon the children's children, unto the third and to the fourth generation.
> —Exodus 34:7, NKJV

The good news is that through Christ, who took all sin on the cross, we have the authority and ability to break these curses and move into freedom for ourselves and our families. It is true that when we accept, profess, and receive Jesus as our Lord and Savior we become born again in our spirit. What is not born again is our soul, which includes our intellect, will, emotions, and ultimately our bodies. Our bodies need restoration. This is why many believers stay bound by generational curses, habits, and addictions after spiritual rebirth. We must intentionally leave generational curses behind as we renew our minds through the Holy Spirit. It was evident that Hemingway was fighting a much darker demon than anyone could see. He was a legend but lived a life of pleasure and sin, and after multiple attempts at suicide and cheating death, death finally won.

As I have learned about illnesses and addictions that can be passed from one generation to the next, I know that everyone is fighting a battle, whether they brought it on by their own actions or they "inherited" it. I don't think Hemingway had hope. I had hope and clung to it! To believe that there is hope for healing and restoration, we have to see past the rubble and the ruin right in front of us! This is not an easy task. It comes down to what we believe, then what we think.

It is the aim of the enemy to incapacitate us in our minds, no matter what the vice or vehicle. If our minds cannot function clearly, the way God intended, then we will not thrive in life bringing glory to Him.

Break Generational Curses

Do you feel like you just can't break a cycle of sin or lack in your life? You can use the prayer below to address generational curses that are hindering your ability to walk victoriously in Christ. If you see a pattern or a struggle that has especially been passed down through generations, this may be an area where you need to focus. Through prayer, the Holy Spirit can change the way you think and set you free. Jesus who died on the cross wants you to share in His wonderful goodness! Let us pray to cleanse our bloodline and take back our legal right:

LORD, as I come into Your Courts and praise Your holy name, I stand before You. LORD, I thank You that what Jesus did for me on the cross now speaks on my behalf before Your Courts. I repent for my own personal sins and transgressions, but I also bring the iniquity of my bloodline to You. I ask that anything the devil would legally accuse me of now be revealed.

Engage with the Holy Spirit

Pray with any knowledge of things that need to be forgiven in your life and in your family's life. Then listen to see if the Holy Spirit speaks or impresses anything else that may be hiding in your or your family's hearts and lives. Pray this prayer as often as you feel led:

> I bring my bloodline to you through my father (name your father) and through my mother (name your mother).

I ask that anything the devil would legally be bringing against me would be known.

I repent of all iniquities I have discerned naturally. (Deal with each issue separately. Go through them one by one, repenting of that which has twisted the bloodline and generations.)

I now ask for the blood of Jesus to speak for me and my bloodline. I ask that any and every legal right of the devil to use these things would now be revoked. Thank You, Lord Jesus, so much for Your blood that speaks for me.

I repent for any and all iniquities I discern in my bloodline through my father and my mother now prophetically. I ask that anything that needs to be exposed in my bloodline would now be seen. Anything the devil, as my legal opponent, would bring against me, I ask that he be made to show it. (Be sensitive at this stage to anything you see, hear, or feel. Anything that is discerned, whether you know about it naturally or not and repent of it.)

I also, Lord, thank You for Colossians 2:14 that declares "You took away every case against me on the cross." I ask, Lord, that anything known or unknown would be removed. I ask that the right of the devil to legally use this against me is now revoked. Thank You so much for nailing all these things against me to Your cross. I receive it and accept in Jesus's name. Amen.

—Robert Henderson,
Prayers and Declarations that Open the Courts of Heaven

Once God issues a verdict of forgiveness and annuls your case in the Courts of Heaven, the case is closed! You now have the authority to address the enemy, tell him that he cannot come back, and close the door on him!

THE ART OF FREEDOM

Freedom Key

Pray, repent, and ask for forgiveness in the Courts of Heaven to receive a verdict from our Heavenly Father and Sovereign Judge that results in cleansing, release, and recompense.

Chapter 8
THE ART OF SURRENDER

I Give Up!

On June 15, 2015, I let go! Spiritually I was tired of feeling like I was throwing punches at the enemy and getting nowhere. I gave up trying to figure things out and doing it my way. I gave up trying to come up with the perfect formula in prayer and daily routine to get my breakthroughs and healing. I gave up pretending that life was good because it wasn't. I broke and in frustration said, "I can't do it, God. I give up trying to be in control and I give you the keys. Would you please forgive me, God, and would you please take over?" This marked the beginning of an incredible journey with God. Life as I had known it—overweight, depressed, chronically ill, and defeated—was about to change drastically in a very good way. All I did to initiate it was surrender!

I wept and questioned Him, "Why, God, why do I feel like You have forsaken me when clearly You say in Your Word that You would never leave me or forsake me?" He said, "I have been waiting for you to ask Me." Every morning from that point on, I made an appointment with God and I just began to be with Him in my "God chair," as my daughter called it. With a cup of coffee and my Bible, I relaxed in my wingback chair that faced the front window where I could watch the rising sun peak over the tree tops. The light danced through the leaves and streamed into my living room the higher the sun got. I read scripture out loud, often accompanied by a devotional. I wrote the scriptures in my journal and then re-read them. I began to create this pattern of read it, write it, and then recite it as a declaration. I played worship music and soaked in the lyrics. Some days I just sat in silence. I did this for months on end! I told God, "I am going to keep coming to this spot each day and not move until You show up!" I, like Jacob, wrestled and would not let go until He blessed me! It sounds a bit demanding, but He was all I had left. Instead of seeking Him first, I had done this last.

I cultivated an abiding lifestyle as I sat with Him, walked with Him, talked with Him, and even drove with Him. My car became a place of peace and a place of worship where I could silence the world around me and share my heart with Him. I continued to journal my thoughts and pour my heart out on paper, surrendering myself and my thoughts daily to make way for Him to make the exchange. He wanted to take my disappointments, doubts, and defeated thinking in exchange for His promises. I began to notice that I never left His presence depressed or sad. There was a marked difference in my daily outlook. I was definitely more positive, and even energetic, after my time in His presence. He was treating my ailments.

Getting to the Heart of the Matter!

One day I sensed a shift in our session. Until this time, He was dealing with the clutter on the surface of my heart and building my trust in Him. Now He really wanted to get to the heart of the matter. He wanted to reveal and heal my hidden, hurting heart.

THE ART OF SURRENDER

Many of us are afraid to trust Him with our heart. We choose to ignore painful issues and sweep them under the rug. Out of sight, out of mind, but not out of God's sight; and your whole being certainly knows that the wound is there. Before long, symptoms begin to manifest from your chronically sick heart, affecting your spirit, mind, and body. I had gotten to this place and living there was hell.

When God created us, "He knew us before we were formed in our mother's womb" (Jeremiah 1:5, NKJV). That is because we were designed in the mind of God—spirit first. And we were created with a soul that He placed in a body, breathing His very breath into us. This is important to understand because it is how all things operate in the Kingdom of God. Everything originates and flows from the Spirit through the soul, then to the body. The spirit, also sometimes referred to as our heart, must be dealt with first. A chronically sick heart that goes untreated can cause hell and hinder heaven in our lives spiritually, mentally, emotionally, and physically. We have to work from the inside out. We must start in the order God intended. His biggest concern is the condition of our hearts.

One by one, the Holy Spirit began to reveal hidden areas of my heart that were wounded by words or actions from others and even myself. As my time with the Lord continued, faces, names, and situations flashed before me; and He let me choose whether I wanted to address it or not. If I chose not to, He would honor that and try again another day. Some days I just wasn't ready to deal with the emotional pain. As my spirit grew stronger in time with Him, I become more willing to allow Him to tackle the delicate condition of my heart.

I will give you a new heart and put a new spirit in you; I will remove from you a heart of stone and give you a heart of flesh.
—Ezekiel 36:26, NIV

This didn't happen every day, but I could see He wanted to clean the house of my heart quickly so He could restore it, and we could move to greater things He had for me. He began to minister to me by speaking instruction and Truth. As the Holy Spirit led me in prayers of forgiveness and blessing for myself and others, the tears would flow. The hurt, jealousy, pride, addiction, anger, and unforgiveness had to go! There was no longer any room for it because He was filling the pain and void with love, disappointments with hope, sadness with joy, and rejection with acceptance.

The Art of Surrender is not about what we are losing but what we will gain according to what the Father wants us to have in the right order, timing, and amount. I can tell you that if anything comes before Him as an idol in our hearts, He will ask you to surrender it. If we do not surrender these things to Him, they will block growth and blessings; and eventually those things will be removed because He is a jealous God.

I realized through many opportunities that partial surrender doesn't cut it with God and is, in fact, disobedience. I see surrender as a way to go from bankrupt to breakthrough; it sets us on our path to freedom and abundant life. We have to be willing to give it to Him, whatever *it* is. I trusted Him enough to take me there; and that is where I began to find healing for my chronically sick heart. The brokenness was being mended and the transformation had begun.

Freedom Key

Start from the inside out and trust Him with your heart. Intentionally be still and yield to the work of the Holy Spirit.

Reflect and Record in Your Journal

As you sit still, quietly ask the Holy Spirit to search your heart and see if there is anything He wants to reveal to you. Wait on the Lord and listen for a word or person's name or watch for a glimpse of an image that might come to mind. Take note of your reaction and begin to talk it out with the Lord. Meditate on the following scripture and look to the promise of what can come from your own personal healing.

> Create in me a clean heart, O God, and renew a steadfast spirit within me. Do not cast me away from Your presence, and do not take your precious Holy Spirit from me. Restore to me the joy of Your salvation and uphold me by Your generous Spirit. Then I will teach transgressors Your ways, and sinners shall be converted to You.
>
> —Psalm 51:10-13, NKJV

Prayer Empowerment

Heavenly Father, in the name of Jesus, I give up! I do not want to govern my own life anymore nor do I want to partially surrender to you. I ask for your mercy and that you would tenderly deal with me as I courageously take a step of faith in trusting you. Holy Spirit, help me to know that you will shine the spotlight on the wounds and areas that need addressed, cleansed and treated. I trust your timing and your healing techniques. I choose to trust you and thank you Jesus that your blood was shed for me to have the hope and fulfillment of full and abundant healing. Today I fully surrender everything to you. Amen.

Chapter 9
The Art of Getting Up

How bad do you want it?

The night Jesus told me to get up at The Crabb Family concert, He meant business. He had work for me to do and His plan for my life was good. He was not going to let His daughter perish. All it took was two words from my Master: "Get up."

A man healed at the pool of Bethesda

¹After this there was a feast of the Jews, and Jesus went up to Jerusalem. ²Now there is in Jerusalem by the Sheep Gate a pool, which is called in Hebrew, Bethesda, having five porches. ³In these lay a great multitude of sick people, blind, lame, paralyzed, waiting for the moving of the water. ⁴For an angel went down at a certain time into the pool and stirred up the water; then whoever stepped in first, after the stirring of the water, was made well of whatever disease he had. ⁵Now a certain man was there who had an infirmity thirty-eight years. ⁶When Jesus saw him lying there, and knew that he already had been in that condition a long time, He said to him, **"Do you want to**

> **be made well?"** ⁷The sick man answered Him, "Sir, I have no man to put me into the pool when the water is stirred up; but while I am coming, others step down before me." ⁸Jesus said to him, **"Rise, take up your bed, and walk."** ⁹And immediately the man was made well, took up his bed, and walked.
>
> —John 5:1-8, NKJV

When I tell my story I often reference the sick man by the pool of Bethesda. In my season of transformation, when opposition arose and the heat intensified, I reminded myself how much I wanted to be healed, whole, and free! I would ask myself "How bad do you want it?"

What is it you are praying and hoping for? The man at the pool kept waiting for someone to help him into the water at the appointed time, but he gave up before his breakthrough. Year after year, he sacrificed what he wanted most and stopped short of his healing. He lived with a defeated mentality for thirty-eight years. Jesus simply asked him if he wanted to be well and the man gave Jesus an excuse. I love how the King James version states that the man was "made whole" as opposed to "healed". The man was not only physically ill but also spiritually blind because he did not know it was the Lord speaking to him. He didn't realize that hope was standing right in front of him! We use an illness mentality to make excuses and eventually the illness identity becomes our reality.

Scripture states that the man would try to make his way down to the water but not make it in time. You would think that the man would stay close to the water where the healings took place, so that the next time the angel came to stir the water he would have a better chance of getting in first. We need to position ourselves for healing so that we are as close as possible to the Living Water, immersing ourselves in it and expecting it to move—just like the man, the angel, and the pool.

I believe the man was made whole the second the Lord engaged with him, but it would have been a disservice to the man had the Lord not given him the opportunity to respond. Jesus allowed the man to operate of his own free will. Even though the man gave an excuse, Jesus still made him whole. But the man had to put forth the effort to get up and walk. When the Healer comes, we have to respond in faith and in action. Our action is our partnering with God to bring forth health and life; and, when we work that out, it becomes the sign that makes people wonder!

The healed man later saw Jesus in the temple. Jesus told him to see that he was well and warned him to sin no more or else something worse would come upon him. I love how Jesus cared enough to find him again and give him further instruction on how to stay well and whole.

It is critical that we choose life with determination, positioning ourselves to encounter the Healer not the Deceiver. The Living Water will grow all God has planted within you in due season, bringing forth healing and fruit.

Gaining Heaven's Perspective for Yourself and Others

The Promise Way of Thinking

I was not living God's best for me and I did not want to continue to be like that man any longer. The Lord heard my cry for help and, in His compassion, He came crashing into my circumstances determined to not let me perish. In the end I had to agree to the invitation and I still had to get up! Getting up was an act of faith and trust. The Holy Spirit empowered me to pick up my mat and walk. His will is always to heal, always! Just like the man at the pool, He saw my destiny and didn't accept my misery.

One encounter with the Lord was all it took for the lame man to receive heaven's destiny for him even though he did not know he was speaking with the Messiah. Jesus proposed a different way of thinking. Jesus knew the man could be whole and He proposed the promise to him. The living and active Word of God was literally at work in that very moment, penetrating the man's heart, mind, and body! This miracle was quick and powerful!

> For the word of God is quick, and powerful, and sharper than any two-edged sword, piercing even to the dividing asunder of soul and spirit, and of the joints and marrow, and is a discerner of the thoughts and intents of the heart.
> —Hebrews 4:12, KJV

You were created in the perfect image of God and He sees you that way. But in our imperfect world our perfect divine design of being is corrupted by the world's perspective. Therefore, we must allow Holy Spirit to renew our minds. "We are to set our minds on things above, living with the mind of Christ adopting heaven's perspective of ourselves and others" (Colossians 3:2-10, NKJV).

God wants you to put on the new man mentality and see yourself the way He does. Seeing life from a heavenly perspective is a foreign concept to many. It requires an unshakeable ability to believe, time in the Word, time in His presence, and the practice of retraining our thought and spoken life.

God is compassion; He has passion for us and wants His people to be whole and prospering in all ways. Almighty God, the Great I AM, showed up to me that night at The Crabb Family concert just as he showed up to the man by the pool of Bethesda. No matter who you are or where you are, His desire is to make you well and whole in Him, and live abundantly as joint heirs to His throne. "He came so we could have life—here and in heaven—and have it abundantly" (John 10:10, NKJV).

The encounters I had with our supernatural God in this season sparked my desire to live again, fueled my belief for healing, and exposed the enemy. My hunger and desire for the word of God grew like crazy in my heart as I continued to seek Him first. It is critical that we choose life with determination, positioning ourselves to encounter the Healer, not the Deceiver. He blesses our obedience when we seek Him first, believe His word, and put action behind our faith The Living Water will grow all that God has planted within you in due season, bringing forth healing, wholeness, and fruit. Decide today that you want to be made well. In Jesus's Name!

Freedom Key

Position yourself to encounter the Healer, not the Deceiver. Be aware and recognize when the Healer is present. Receive and agree to God's way of thinking.

Reflect and Record in Your Journal

Take a moment to reflect. Do you want to be made well? Is there an area of your life where you need to partner with God to see His promises delivered to you? Record these in your journal and talk to God about it! Listen and then record what He says. Ask God what that would require from you. Then pick up your mat and walk!

Read It, Write It, Recite It, Repeat!

Find several supporting scriptures that would be considered "The Promise" to your problem, whether it is physical, financial, emotional, relational, or something else. Write these scriptures, recite them out loud, and meditate on them continually as you pray them in supplication to God. Nothing is more powerful than praying the Word of God! Ask Holy Spirit to reveal to you the source of the problem. Then ask for His wisdom for how to move forward out of it.

Believe the Promise and expect an answer. Expect the Promise! Continue to apply this practice as you communicate and cultivate your relationship with the Lord, walking it in faith with action.

> *Jesus said to him, "If you can believe, all things are possible to him who believes."*
>
> —Mark 9:23, NKJV

Prayer Empowerment

Heavenly Father, In the name of Jesus, I repent for excuses, an illness mentality, or victim mentality that has left me wanting to give up or leave this life before your timing. I receive your forgiveness for any acts or thoughts I've had regarding giving up on life and the hope of Jesus. Holy Spirit help me to stay positioned by the Living Water in order to stay close to my life-giving source, You. I pray God BREAK OFF any spirits of infirmity plaguing my body and mind through generational bloodline curses or any sin I have allowed in my life. I ask Holy Spirit to come and seal any deliverance or healing that takes place fully filling this temple for you. Lord, I ask to help me pick up my mat so I can live for You and bring glory and honor to You. Amen.

PART THREE

The Art of Renewing the Soul: Be Transformed by Renewing Your Mind

Chapter 10
THE ART OF RENEWING THE MIND

Recognition Is Ammunition

Visual imagery has a great impact and influence on my understanding. That may seem backwards to an analytical person but it's how I've always operated. In 2014 I was invited to a local ladies' Bible study. The woman who invited me was like a spiritual mother to me and she was convinced that the book they were about to study would help me. She felt that my illnesses were linked to toxic thinking. The book was *Who switched off your brain?* by Dr. Caroline Leaf. I quickly began to see what was sabotaging me. The Lord used the teachings in the book to expose the enemy in my life. That enemy was toxic thinking! The author had aligned scientific information with scripture. That fascinated me. As I continued the study of Dr. Leaf's resources, I learned startling statistics that shockingly lined up with my situation. I was learning just how toxic and deadly my thought life was.

> Research is now proving that 75% to 95% of the illnesses that plague us today are a direct result of our thought

life. What we think about affects us physically and emotionally. It's an epidemic of toxic emotions. As well as there are INTELLECTUAL and MEDICAL reasons to FORGIVE!

—Dr. Caroline Leaf "Controlling Your Toxic Thoughts"

This was me! I was sick mentally, emotionally, and physically! I held onto a scripture passage by the Apostle John that gave me hope. I had to figure out how this scripture and others could become my reality.

> Beloved, I pray that in every way you may succeed and prosper in all things and be in good health (physically), just as your soul prospers (spiritually). For I was greatly pleased when (some of the) brothers came to me and testified to your faithfulness to the truth, that is, how you are walking in truth. I have no greater joy than this, to hear that my (spiritual) children are living (their lives) in the truth.
>
> —3 John 2:2-4, AMP

The visuals in Dr. Leaf's book were the clincher for me. For the first time in my life I saw an image of what my brain looked like when healthy or negative thoughts came in, and it shocked me! Dr. Leaf's image was something that I truly could relate to—life and death—and it was now etched into my mind!

Visually, a brain that is fed a healthy thought resembles a tree in full bloom. A brain that is fed a negative thought resembles a leafless tree with no fruit. This was startling to me. I now had a visual to help me catch and corral my thoughts. One day after seeing the visual analogy, I was at a traffic light and a negative self-worth thought entered my mind. Immediately I was able to stop and block it. I continued to seek the Holy Scriptures for truth to defeat the barrage of lies that would come. The more often I could catch and corral them, the less they came. The enemy was losing ground in my mind.

Thought Corralling and Journaling
What Exactly Does It Mean to Take Every Thought Captive?

Envision in your mind that you are holding a lasso and as thoughts come, invited or intrusive, you swing your lasso and capture all the thoughts within it, corralling them into one place. God gave me this vision one morning as I sat still with him and my journal, about to "empty" my mind and thoughts on paper. He said He didn't want me to empty my mind as much as He wanted me to surrender my thoughts to Him.

God wants us to surrender negative thoughts and exchange them for true and healthy ones. We need to make room for the Holy Spirit to speak and fill us with His thoughts, desires, and instructions. Vision is like a powerful locomotive when we engage it properly it can move and steer us in the right direction. Recognition will be our greatest ammunition when acted upon properly and aligned with the Word of God. We have to recognize the thoughts, pain, disappointments, and victories; and process them properly. When we sit to corral our thoughts in one place, we have the ability to expose the source by recognizing them. What we do after recognizing them is up to us. We can allow our thoughts to injure us or we can use them as ammunition to find freedom and remain free. I often tell people the fight to stay free is harder than the fight to get free. Once we find and understand the strategies God has given us to remain free, we can then walk in trust and rest that He will be fighting for us. There will always be a fight to remain free as long as we are on this side of Heaven.

Instead of emptying my thoughts, I corralled them and placed them at the feet of Christ and the lap of the Father. I was able to give them to Him and seek Holy Spirit to help me find a better thought, a right and true thought. I would practice this as I incorporated meditating on the Word of God and aligning my thoughts with scripture. It was during the study of Dr. Leaf's book that I came to understand how to partner with Holy Spirit and allow Him to renew my mind. Journaling became a big part of this process. Through journaling, we can do what I call "corral, reframe, and reclaim" our thoughts.

The word of God tells us that we have to do this. It must be a continual and daily exercise. The Amplified Bible states

> And do not be conformed to this world [any longer with its superficial values and customs], but be transformed and progressively changed [as you mature spiritually] by the renewing of your mind [focusing on godly values and ethical attitudes], so that you may prove [for yourselves] what the will of God is, that which is good and acceptable and perfect [in His and purpose for you].
>
> —Romans 12:2, AMP

There are natural patterns—both good and bad—that will tell you how you think, believe, and operate. We need to be aware of these patterns in our life and observe our actions that follow them. When we take responsibility for our thought life and make an effort to change, the Holy Spirit steps in to help.

Freedom Key

Recognize, corral, reframe, and reclaim your thoughts. Be mindful of what you think and say; take every thought captive and bring it into obedience with what Christ says. Replace negative self-talk with God's truth. Your words have power for good or evil.

THE ART OF RENEWING THE MIND

Death and life are in the power of the tongue, and those who love it will eat its fruit.

—Psalm 18:21, NKJV

Prayer Empowerment

Heavenly Father, in the name of Jesus, I confess and repent that I do not always take my thoughts captive. Thank you that I have been given the mind of Christ when I received you into my heart. I pray for a spirit of discernment to help recognize what is not your greatest thoughts towards me. Forgive me for ever speaking against myself out of ill thoughts and offending the workmanship of your hands. Help me to discern between good thoughts that bring life and evil thoughts that destroy the very nature of You within me. Help me to be more vigilant to take my thoughts captive and bring them into obedience with what You say. As I read your word, Holy Spirit please renew my mind to think, respond, and act like Christ. Thank you for sanctifying my thoughts and my imagination in Your precious name. Amen.

Chapter 11
THE ART OF POSSESSING PEACE

Do the Next Right Thing!

Part of the process of being renewed in our minds is having a check and balance system. This helps us weigh the source of our thoughts. You can check and balance everything with God's Word and His way of doing things. It is a plumb line. If something doesn't line up, ask the Holy Spirit to illuminate the culprit that has you off center. This is an important practice to learn as you begin to recognize thought sources, determine right actions, and make right decisions that generate growth. You need to know your center or plumb line to successfully and victoriously walk out your journey in wisdom and peace.

You can develop a plumb-line system to gauge your peace levels. When faced with decisions, my husband and I pray together and individually seek the Lord. We then come together to talk about it. If one or both of us did not have complete peace over the situation we do not proceed forward. We believe it is easier to wait and go forward later than to go backwards after making a not-so-good decision. We have never regretted waiting to decide when it came to our peace.

In art, plumb lines are undeviating vertical lines used as a reference to determine alignment. It is crucial for us to be aligned with our Source so we have the right perspective to make the right decision. If we are unaligned, everything else in our lives will be off.

Several years ago, I had to make a big decision and had forgotten my peace plumb-line system. It needed to be the right decision. I was struggling to find peace in the midst of the situation. The decision involved a decent sum of money and I had to consider the emotional, physical, and mental demands it would put on my family and myself.

I explained my situation to a dear friend, who was very much a seasoned saint. After I shared the dilemma, she simply said with a quiet and confident voice, "Do the next right thing." Her statement immediately resonated with me. There was something about how she used the word "right" in the context of my decision that seemed right! I had forgotten to check my peace plumb line and was agonizing over what to do. My thoughts ran away from me into "what ifs" and "if only" statements. We are good at writing the story before we consult with the Author of our story. The Lord desires us to seek Him first and make wise decisions according to what is right.

She had given me my answer without technically telling me what to do. You could say I was after a "best yes" decision. I immediately felt peace and clarity come to me as the Holy Spirit confirmed the situation. You might ask, how did I know it was Holy Spirit? Because God is the author of Peace and Satan is the author of confusion, and I was experiencing peace! God never meant for us to walk this journey alone and He strategically places people in our path to provide wise counsel when needed. We should never have to agonize over anything because we have the Word of God as our foundational guide, which is right and true. Secondly, we have the greatest wise helper of all, Holy Spirit. When you put those two together,

Spirit and Word, you have the Dynamic Duo! The Holy Spirit is the one that illuminates our path. The Word of God is our path, the Holy Spirit illuminates it.

We have to make decisions that are right for ourselves and our families no matter what others say. You may risk loss when you go against others' opinions, but the reward for following God and His way of doing things is much greater. By doing the next right thing I made a "best yes" decision and my peace plumb line was restored.

The Holy Spirit Traffic Light

When my kids were little and learning to understand traffic lights, we would sing a song I created to help them remember the meaning of the color of the traffic lights. It goes like this: "Red means STOP, yellow means SLOW, green means GO, GO, GO, GO!" And we would repeat it a few times to a made-up tune. I would listen to the voice of my little tykes in the back seat continue singing until it trailed off into a whisper. As they grew older and began to come into the understanding of the Holy Spirit, I used this traffic light illustration as a way to help them make decisions according to God's word and His desired will for them. I was teaching them the art of possessing peace by making right decisions.

Romans 8:28 tells us, "And we know God causes all things to work together for good to those who love God, to those who are called according to his purpose." (NASB)

I believe that it is always a green GO light when you are walking in close relationship with the Holy Spirit until He changes the signal. If the signal is not clear, the problem is not the signal, the problem is the connection. When we are close to someone and spend time with them, we can begin to determine what they may say and do. The same goes with God. As we cultivate our relationship with Him, learn from His Word and how He operates, the signal becomes clearer and we begin to recognize when it changes. As He is raising us in His ways, He begins to trust us enough to make the right decision. When He sees us going off course, He will warn us and direct us back to the right path. When we walk with Him, He orchestrates and navigates our path. What seems normal to us may seem illogical or even irrational to others. As a true Jesus follower in society today, we will be watched, examined, and criticized. Do not worry because God is right there waiting for us to look at His traffic signal and He wants to give us His "Yes and amen" approval!

When I share the traffic light teaching with young and older adults, they snicker and think it is a childish concept, but there is a reason God says to be childlike. He doesn't mean childish, but childlike in wonder and belief. God's way is simple and practical. I use this clearly outlined concept when equipping others in the way of Spirit filled living. When they apply the keys of the teaching and work with the Holy Spirit, they possess peace in their everyday decision making.

God inspires and leads, but we were created to co-labor with Him and contribute from our unique make-up that He placed within us. Making decisions, good or not so good, is all part of the journey to become like Christ. These are keys to making right, wise, practical, and peace-filled decisions.

It really is an art. As with creating any art, there are factors to consider, components that are needed, and a process that is applied—which is often messy—to do the next right thing! This requires practice and connection with the Holy Spirit.

There will be times that we will miss it. The goal is for fewer misses as we grow closer to Him. I like to think that our misses are more like "happy accidents," as the late Bob Ross called them. If God says that He can cause all things to work together for good for us who love Him then even if we miss it, He can still use it!

Apply the right keys, check your peace plumb line and you will be on your way to making right decisions according to the heart of God. These decision-making keys can silence agonizing and anxious thoughts in your head and bring peace to your heart and mind. More importantly, when we make right decisions with right motives, we keep Satan from spewing accusations against us and our character. A pure heart led by pure motives according to God's word will silence the enemy. As you make decisions, pray this prayer:

> Search me, O God, and know my heart; Try me, and know my anxieties;
> And see if there is any wicked way in me, and lead me in the way everlasting.
> —Psalm 139:23-24, NKJV

Meditate on the following scripture passage and seek Him first as you develop your peace plumb line and watch for those traffic signals.

> Trust in the Lord with all your heart and lean not on your own understanding;
> In all your ways acknowledge Him, And He shall direct your path.
> —Proverbs 3:5-6, NKJV

Freedom Key

Make right decisions with pure motives. Watch for the Holy Spirit's Traffic Light signals. Follow His promptings. Peace of mind brings freedom.

Reflect and Record in Your Journal

Have you seen the Holy Spirit Traffic Light work in your life? If so, did you know it was the Holy Spirit trying to direct you? How did you respond? How will you respond now that you understand how He works? Share a time when you "saw" a signal to Go, Slow, or Stop.

Prayer Empowerment

Holy Spirit awaken and sharpen my spiritual senses to hear, know, and feel when you are leading and guiding me. Help me to be quick to see and obey Your Holy Spirit traffic light signal. I pray that you give me peace in the moments I need to take the next right step and trust that you will bring further confirmation when it is Your voice. I trust You as You lead me into all truth. In the name of Jesus, Amen.

Chapter 12
The Art of Being Transformed

The Holy Spirit Is the Missing Link!

There is a term that describes the true inner change we have after being with the Living God. *Metanoia* is a Greek term that defines repentance and a full turning and changing of our inner being. This term describes the way that we are transformed by the Holy Spirit. This experience could also be considered as a day of great awakening in one's life. That day in the Catholic church when I encountered the living God wasn't a true metanoia experience, but it did cause me to seek Him more.

Metanoia theologically defined

> The transliteration of the Greek defines *metanoia* as a transformative change of heart that drives the changing of the mind, stemming from *metanoéō*; the act of repentance to completely turn from the current state of thought or action (*meta* meaning "after, with" and *noéō* "to perceive, to think").
>
> —Wikipedia, Strong's Concordance

THE ART OF BEING TRANSFORMED

One morning after I was off my prescription medications and thinking clearly again, I was between sleep and waking, and I heard the Holy Spirit speak. It was purely one of those mystery revelations delivered to your doorstep. He said, "One cannot have metanoia without the baptism of the Holy Spirit!" He repeated himself until I sat up in my bed, documented what He had said, and began to pray into His message. I knew this was important and remember feeling like I was about to find the treasure from a clue in a scavenger hunt! I knew what "metanoia" meant in both the English and Greek context; but why was He telling me about the baptism of the Holy Spirit? I had personally experienced metanoia in my own life and was living out of my changed and renewed mind. I had been saved, water baptized as a baby and an adult. I also had multiple encounters of being *with* Holy Spirit; but what was this link He wanted to be sure I knew? He repeated the original message again and revealed even more, but this time in a very firm, direct voice, "You cannot have a true metanoia without an encounter with Me and the baptism of the Holy Spirit! It is not *you* who changes the way you think; it is *I*, Holy Spirit."

He proceeded to explain that it was our responsibility to partner with Him to renew our minds daily by hearing the message and reading the Holy word; but it is He who drives our soul to a place of metanoia and changes the mind.

He said, "After the initial baptism, daily conversation and continual walking with Him keeps us in a renewed mind, and metanoia happens continually at greater levels. Continual fellowship with Holy Spirit keeps our minds pure and changed and keeps our spirits free from oppression! This continual process is rooted in LOVE from the Father to make us into His likeness!"

He was blowing my mind! He made it clear as to what the outcome would be when we continue in our obedience of daily and intentional fellowship with Him after the baptism *with* Him. We are always growing in God so we will not stagnate. Instead we will be continually renewed and changed at greater levels! That excites me! There is no end to Him! I was then directed to these supporting scriptures quoting John the Baptist.

> "As for me, I baptize you with water because of (your) repentance (that is, because you are willing to change your inner self, your old way of thinking, regret your sin, and live a changed life), that He (the Messiah) who is coming after me is mightier (more powerful, more noble) than I, whose sandals I am not worthy to remove (even as his slave); He will baptize you (who truly repent) with the Holy Spirit and (you who remain unrepentant with fire (judgment)."
>
> —Matthew 3:11, AMP

The phrase "truly repent" was exactly what Holy Spirit was saying to me and He was calling it "true metanoia": a true repentance, a changed way of being that drives the soul to be renewed.

I realized that apart from the Holy Spirit and His baptism we cannot change anything by ourselves. We must do our part, surrender our hearts and souls to Him, actively capturing thoughts and applying truth so He can work and bring forth the change. Romans 12:2 says, "Do not conform to the pattern of this world but be transformed by the renewing of your mind." It is impossible for us to transform ourselves; that is why we need the baptism of the Holy Spirit! This scripture has a command followed by a promise. The command is "do not conform to the world's ways." The promise and reward for committing to and following through with that is "you will be transformed." That transformation comes in two ways: by conforming to God's ways instead of to the world, and by allowing Holy Spirit to renew our mind with His power and words of truth.

I never once thought I needed to be transformed—healed, yes—but I never prayed, "God transform me." This tells me that we desperately need a new understanding of what it means to be truly repentant, saved, baptized, and walking in the Spirit with a kingdom mind not a carnal mind. I am passionate about helping people understand this truth. This is a very important key to our freedom!

The Baptism of the Holy Spirit

A very large number of believers live with strongholds in their minds and limp around without the baptism and power of the Holy Spirit. We may be a born-again believer of Jesus, but if we have not been baptized by the Holy Spirit we are missing out on so much of what God has for us. In Acts 19, Paul encounters believers who had not heard of the Holy Spirit. They had only received the baptism of repentance and didn't understand what he was saying; but when he explained it, they did not resist and were baptized when Paul laid hands on them to receive.

> *1* And it happened, while Apollos was at Corinth, that Paul, having passed through the upper regions, came to Ephesus. And finding some disciples
> *2* he said to them, "Did you receive the Holy Spirit when you believed?"
> So, they said to him, "We have not so much as heard whether there is a Holy Spirit."
> *3* And he said to them, "Into what then were you baptized?"
> So, they said, "Into John's baptism."
> *4* Then Paul said, "John indeed baptized with a baptism of repentance, saying to the people that they should believe on Him who would come after him, that is, on Christ Jesus."

⁵ When they heard this, they were baptized in the name of the Lord Jesus.

⁶ And when Paul had laid hands on them, the Holy Spirit came upon them, and they spoke with tongues and prophesied.

⁷ Now the men were about twelve in all.

⁸ And he went into the synagogue and spoke boldly for three months, reasoning and persuading concerning the things of the kingdom of God.

—NKJV Biblegateway.com

Paul was a willing vessel for the Holy Spirit; the believers manifested their baptism by speaking in tongues and prophesying. Both are gifts of the Holy Spirit's ministry. When Paul continued on his journey in verse 8, he went "in boldness." This is another sign and characteristic of the presence and baptism of the Holy Spirit.

Jesus was baptized with the Holy Spirit before He performed miracles, healed the sick, cast out demons, and walked in power to defeat the temptations of the enemy in the wilderness. He had to have the baptism of the Holy Spirit to walk to his physical death and withstand the act of crucifixion for us. If Christ needed to be baptized in the Holy Spirit, then we do, too!

This baptism comes by way of surrender and yielding. If we have received Jesus and are a professing believer of Him then we already have everything we need within us. We have received the fullness of God and the Holy Spirit dwells within us. The Holy Spirit works from the inside out, so the baptism of the Holy Spirit comes from within. External baptism in water is a public profession of our belief in Jesus Christ as our Lord and Savior. The Spirit always works from the inside out; and Satan always works from the outside in to influence the believer. Like Paul, one can release the baptism blessing, but the work is done by the Holy Spirit. This is how we are clothed with power from within.

Through the act of being born-again in our spirit we are adopted into the family of God by the Holy Spirit. It is then that we become a child of God. Our souls must be renewed as we grow and mature in Christ. The baptism of the Holy Spirit is nothing to fear nor is there a perfect prayer or formula for it.

Could you be preventing the baptism of the Holy Spirit in your life? There may be a stronghold of false doctrinal beliefs that need to be broken in order for you to operate in your spiritual gifts, particularly your prayer language of tongues. The most common stronghold to prevent you from releasing your spiritual gifts is the religious spirit which is linked to a belief that the Holy Spirit's gifts have ceased and are not for today. That is a false belief system and must be broken and replaced with truth. Lots of truth! If this spirit is operating in your life you can break that by repenting for agreeing to it, renouncing the false belief and asking the Holy Spirit to reveal truth to you. Then proceed to ask the Holy Spirit to baptize you in order for you to release your new gift and weapon through your spirit and mouth!

Here are four areas you can examine in your life to see if something is blocking the spiritual gifts from flowing in your life.

- Are you overthinking it? Surrender your intellect. Being analytical will quench the Spirit.
- Are you being prideful or having preconceived ideas?
- Are you fearful of what you will look like? Do not be superficial when it comes to the fullness of your faith. Who cares what people think when it is for our King! Fear and doubt are the enemy's primary way to keep it bound within you.

- Surrender and yield your will. You must act in partnership with God to speak what the Spirit is putting on your tongue! You may experience an utterance or a boldness to speak out.

- Are you resisting? Obedience to the Holy Spirit in the moment is key for this to flow and grow!

Prayer Application

Prayer and worship are powerful ways to usher us into God's presence. If you are born again and want to experience the baptism of the Holy Spirit you can pray right now where you are! As you seek His face, welcome Holy Spirit and surrender to Him. Submit and yield to the work He will do in and through you to accomplish God's will. Repent to cleanse your spirit and your soul. If you said yes to any of the prior points, then repent. Pray this prayer of surrender in faith:

Father, thank You for Your promise to pour out Your spirit on all flesh in the last days according to Joel chapter 2:28. I surrender all of me to You, and submit my intellect, my will, and my emotions to You today. I am desiring to release the supernatural gifts of the Holy Spirit. In the name of Jesus, I ask you to baptize me in the Holy Spirit. I receive these gifts now by faith. Awaken every dormant gift within me and let it pour out of me like rivers of living water. I want all that You have for me. I ask that You release from me now my prayer language and the gifts of the Holy Spirit for Your glory and purposes of the Kingdom. Thank You, Lord. Amen.

Be still and engage with the Spirit as you wait for Him to move and release from within you, fulfilling the baptism. Begin to put praise on your lips and speak, "Hallelujah, hallelujah, hallelujah." With palms open or arms lifted high continue to praise and thank Him out loud. Allow the Holy Spirit to speak through you and do not resist. You may feel a sensation come over you of electrical power, or a surge of boldness and praise bubble up from within you—a sudden burst of joy. You may begin to tremble or weep. No reaction is wrong when it is the Holy Spirit.

When the gift of tongues begins to manifest you may begin to hear foreign sounding syllables forming. As you continue in praise open up your mouth and speak what you hear! It may only be a few sha sha sha's or da da da's or a mix of both or other syllable sounds. Everyone's prayer language will be different but sound similar. Yours will be unique to you. Just like we all have different sounding voices from our God given vocal cords, so it will be with your gift of tongues. It is *your* heavenly voice. Begin to take notice of any new gifting and empowering spiritual changes. After your time with Him, journal and document your experience. Pray and exercise your gifts daily. This will help them grow in maturity.

Freedom Key

Seek and ask for the baptism of the Holy Spirit. Surrender, asking in faith with expectation, then exercise it daily. Obedience to the Holy Spirit's promptings in the moment are key!

Reflect and Record in Your Journal

Journal and document your experiences. I would love for you to contact me through my email at www.theartoffreedombook.com and tell me your experiences after seeking and praying this prayer. I'm excited to share in your blessings.

Chapter 13
The Art of Being Online

Scroll Responsibly

Above all else, guard your heart, for it is the wellspring of life.
—Proverbs 4:23, NIV

Where were you on February 4, 2004? This was the day that nineteen-year-old Harvard sophomore, Mark Zuckerberg, launched the social media platform "thefacebook.com." As of December 31, 2018, Facebook had 2.32 billion monthly active users. That is 30% of the earth's known population! That opens enormous potential for both positive and toxic information to enter our lives. People are hungry for connection. With the touch of a finger you can connect with anyone around the world or around the block. Now with the visual platform Instagram on the rise, the intake of information is not only registering as a thought but also as an image, doubling the opportunity for good or bad results. Social media is not evil; however, as with any tool, it is what we do with it that leads to a good or bad outcome. It is a place to share your wins, post vacation pictures, announce important moments in life, and sometimes even let out a rant or two.

Social interactions, peer pressure, bullying, and comparing ourselves to others can make us feel devalued, unattractive, and unsuccessful. It can rob us of our very identity if we do not guard it. Possessing peace is needed now more than ever as we are living in a society with an abundance of uninvited noise pollution that causes information overload. My use of social media led to anxiety, depression, and social idolization. Not only was I a prisoner in my mind and physical body, but I slowly began to feel like a prisoner in my own home. The anxiety and depression continued for eight long years with sleepless nights, debilitating physical pain, migraines, panic attacks, chronic fatigue, and weight gain until I stopped and took a social media fast.

I needed my joy back! No amount of wishing or repetitive scriptural declaring would change anything without identifying the root cause and dealing with it in faith and action. Dr. Caroline Leaf states that not recognizing, or denying, our present situation is harmful to the make-up of our brain. If our belief is off, then true brain and life change cannot happen. She compares a positive affirmation to a Band-Aid. She states that if a positive affirmation is not done properly it will not work. We have to find the core reason why we are having to say the affirmation to truly change our brain and renew our mind.

When you spend countless hours absorbing the drama and information from others' lives, you are not renewing your mind in the right way. Seek to know and understand the knowledge of God's Word and anything the Holy Spirit leads you to want to learn.

> [7] The instruction of the Lord is perfect, renewing one's life; the testimony of the Lord is trustworthy, making the inexperienced wise.

⁸The precepts of the Lord are right, making the heart glad; the command of the Lord is radiant, making the eyes light up.

⁹ The fear of the Lord is pure, enduring forever; the ordinances of the Lord are reliable and altogether righteous.

¹⁰ They are more desirable than gold—than an abundance of pure gold; and sweeter than honey dripping from a honeycomb.

¹¹ In addition, your servant is warned by them, and in keeping them there is an abundant reward.

—Psalm 19:7-11, CSB

FASTING FROM THE ENEMY
A Social Media, Media, and Social Sabbatical

I had just started seeing a spirit-filled Christian counselor for anxiety, depression, and my self-worth issues. I literally felt like my life was spinning out of control and it was not well with my soul. Have you ever seen spiral waterslides where the only way out is the big black hole in the middle? That is how I envisioned my life at the time. Life was definitely spinning me around and around. As the demands of life and the drama of social media intensified, my expectations of myself rose even higher. I began to take control and manage my social media feed more closely so I wouldn't feel overwhelmed or suffocated by so many posts. I couldn't process the onslaught of information, so my husband suggested I take a break from social media. I considered it and asked my counselor what she thought. She encouraged me to do so. I was keeping a journal of my mental and emotional health issues as they arose. Going through the journaling motions, I was surprised to see change happen three days after my "social sabbatical" began. I called it a "social sabbatical" but God would soon speak and inform me that I was fasting. He assured me that He would honor the "soul fast" and bless me in return. This gave the whole event a new meaning and fueled my ability to abstain. The following is a journal entry from that day.

July 15, 2015 – My Social Sabbatical. I started the fb and social fast! Dealing with anxiety, depression, and chronic physical pain. Today God revealed to me that this thing I was calling a social sabbatical that I started as an experiment was actually a fast. He said that He was going to bless me for sacrificing those things in return for the time I was spending with Him and in His word. He has been moving in amazing ways on my behalf and opening doors because of it. I now know it was ordained by Him, but I didn't recognize it at first. I thought it was my idea to do this—get off of Facebook, Instagram, disconnect with people by email and Twitter, and limit my TV time and phone usage with meaningless conversation. I decided I would focus on me and Him. I would invest in me, searching for me again in Him. Taking back the things that the Enemy had stolen from me through illness, including finances, purpose, and peace of mind. I was setting things right in the Courts of Heaven and repenting for the things I did to bring my condition on and searching my ancestry bloodline. I am reclaiming the things I had given up. I am asking God to reawaken dreams again. Bringing back prayers and desires that had been pressed down, pushed down deep in my soul and forgotten. I am learning to yearn for His presence, just spending time with Him silently. Loving on Him and letting Him love on me. Finding my strengths and my weaknesses and allowing Him to be my strength in that weakness. Praising Him in the times of pain that I feel that pain knowing that I'm alive, full and well, alive to feel the pain. And being able to celebrate the victory of overcoming it with Him when it passes. For He is faithful to help us endure through the hardship. In the beginning of this social sabbatical I was feeling bad and guilty because I abruptly stopped contact with people and communication on Facebook. I did make a notice on my art page that I would not be doing any more classes or taking any more orders for the summer until further notice but that was it. I was nervous that people were going to be upset with me. I was fearing man more than God. But I was afraid that if I opened the door and contacted one person or another person it would just ruin my quiet and my recovery process. It would ruin that time, that 'bubble' so to speak, that I had created with being alone with Him. I needed a break. I was overwhelmed mentally, emotionally, and physically. But I was underwhelmed spiritually. I needed to underwhelm my schedule and what I was reading daily and putting in front of me and spending my time on, and instead overwhelm my spirit to find my center, Christ, and bring my plumb line back to balance again. I needed to learn to love life again and not dread it. I was feeling guilty because I wasn't responding to emails, I wasn't returning phone messages, and I wasn't responding to texts at all or at least not right away. I just couldn't. I still felt I was fragile, and my heart would fall to pieces again. I had just kind of dropped off the face of the earth and did away with certain social media groups that stressed me out and submerged myself in Him, His word, painting, music, meditation and prayer. I didn't become a hermit. I still went out, I just became very choosy with whom I was in contact, with what I watched, what I listened to, and what I decided to allow into my world. I put up very strict boundaries for me. I felt like I had invisible reins on me like I couldn't pick the phone up to call somebody or email someone or return a text. It wasn't me doing it, it was the Spirit, it was God saying, "No, I will not allow you to do that, not yet," and it was at that time that I realized that this was not me choosing to do this, that it was God! He had me in this place, He had brought me to this place of renewing, searching, refreshing. I had found my green pasture again.

For over a decade I had gotten used to saying "yes" to everyone's demands and feeling like I had to in order to be a good Christian, but I was sabotaging myself. It had to stop, and this was how I broke the cycle during my fast. At the same time that I was seeing the counselor, a very valuable book sat on my shelf waiting for me to crack it open, *The Best Yes* by Lysa Terkeurst. I was amazed at the content and how it resonated so deeply with my soul and lined up with my life. I was going to stop being a people pleaser once and for all. Lysa listed out the *Best Yes* categories: physical, financial, spiritual, and emotional. She explained that if it wasn't a "yes" across the board, then it was a "no." I took *The Best Yes* principles and expanded on them. I had to add "mentally" to the list since I suffered from so many challenges linked to my thought life. It became my checklist for making decisions. If it wasn't physically, financially, spiritually, emotionally, and mentally a "yes," then it was a "no." Lysa brilliantly explains that if we don't change the way we make decisions we will continue to end up with the same results, and the decisions you make determine the schedule you keep. I definitely needed a wiser and more life-generating schedule!

My fast went on for three months. I experienced rapid results on a whole-person level from the spirit-filled counseling, my fasting, and dedicating time to the Lord in prayer and painting. When the time came to reenter society, I told my counselor that I was afraid I would lose all I had gained over the last three months with the Lord. I liked the life we had created, and I was thriving. She assured me that God's timing was perfect and that He would not take from me what He had given. She said, "He has shored up your foundations and has made you capable of facing life in society again." I knew she was right, but I was still nervous. I had to take a step of faith and trust that He would keep me in all my ways as I ventured back out into society.

My identity and worth in Christ had been restored, joy had returned, my perception of myself had changed, and I had a new perspective on life. Not to mention my weight began to rapidly come off and, in no time, I lost 40 pounds and eliminated the last of my prescriptions, eventually resulting in a total of 80 pounds lost. I felt empowered and happy! He had renewed my entire soul, not just my mind in those three months.

> Walk in the wisdom toward those who are outside, redeeming the time. Let your speech always be with grace, seasoned with salt, you may know how you ought to answer each one.
>
> —Colossians 4:5-6, NKJV

Freedom Key

Limit your time on social media and unnecessary media. Choose wisely where you spend your time in social settings. Replace old habits and incorporate a new way of living by learning God's Word, listening to kingdom-equipping and life-enriching podcasts, and spending intentional time with Him in prayer and worship or creative activity. Seek God's counsel and His wisdom to make the next right decision! Choose clean music and humor to laugh daily!

My "Best Yes" Checklist

Ask yourself: Does it generate life and peace in all these areas?

Spiritually—Does it align with scripture and the heart of God?
Physically—Does it overtax or overcommit any of these areas: body, house, or family?

Financially—Does is put a strain on your finances; is it being a good steward?
Emotionally—Does it stress you out and negatively affect you, causing dread, depression, or anxiety?
Mentally—Does it overtax you mentally? Is it healthy or toxic to your brain/thought life?

All of these affect our mental state and physical bodies, hindering our ability to function well in everyday life.

Reflect and Record in Your Journal

Evaluate your relationship with social media platforms, social groups, TV, and music, paying attention to emotions and thought patterns. What do you need restored—love, joy, peace, etc.? Ask the Holy Spirit to help you determine what should stay and what should go. Then ask Him to help you manage that time, setting up strict boundaries for yourself.

Meditate on Proverbs 4:23: "Above all else, guard your heart, for it is the wellspring of life." (NIV)

Apply your spiritual and emotional findings. Write out a promise to yourself for how you will guard your heart and mind incorporating what you observed in evaluation and meditation. Above all be kind to yourself. Recognize that restoration is a process.

Prayer Empowerment

Heavenly Father, in the name of Jesus, I repent for allowing comparison to steal from my identity, my peace, my purpose, my worth and joy. I want to only have my identity, peace, purpose, worth and joy found in you. I receive all these from you today. Holy Spirit help me to discipline my actions, thoughts, and activity on social media and in social settings. Help me to arrest thoughts immediately as they try to come and steal from me according to John 10:10. I pray, Holy Spirit guard my heart and mind as we are subjected to so much information overload and noise in this world. Help me to see myself as you see me and love myself as You love me according to Psalm 139. Holy Spirit be a constant voice in my life helping me to make Best Yes© decisions for my life. I praise you for I am fearfully and wonderfully made and there is no one else like me. Thank you for giving me life, identity, worth and purpose. Amen.

Chapter 14
THE ART OF GUARDING YOUR GATE

Knock, Knock, Who's There?

My four-pound teacup Chihuahua Zoey does not know that she is tiny. She is as fearless as a lion. I admire her courage and learn a lesson or two from the fact that she is not intimidated by size or looks. She is secure in her identity. She will not wait until someone enters the property to alert me. She goes on guard even if someone is crossing the street. I have to assure her that I have heard her and am acting accordingly. She will not rest until the intruder is taken care of or gone. I liken this to the gift of discernment that we can receive through the Holy Spirit as we guard our minds and our hearts.

Visualize your home as a series of court areas. Your property line to the door is the outer court. The foyer is the inner court and acts as a gate. The interior of your home is your most intimate court that you would protect at all costs. There is a knock at the door. The dog barks to let you know someone is there. You were not expecting anyone, so you look through the peephole for safety. What you do next will determines what enters your home. This is key to guarding your "gate" and making sure that nothing enters and harms your prized place. You have the ability and right to not open that door. Listen to your spirit and see what color traffic light the Holy Spirit gives you: red, yellow, or green. Once you open the door and allow someone or something to enter, you have to work twice as hard to remove it or escort it out.

I have been known to talk to people through the wooden door or ignore the uninvited guest all together. I am not living in fear but instead using wisdom and discernment.

The house metaphor illustrates what the act of guarding our hearts and minds looks like. The Enemy is out to destroy us and wants to trap us in our minds where we become entangled with lies. Simply said, there is a war over our souls, and we must be vigilant to protect it! If we don't guard our mind, will, and emotions they will become a place where strongholds are erected. The Enemy can spiritually paralyze us and render us ineffective. You may have heard the saying "Don't give the devil an inch" but I say, "Don't even crack that door!" We do not want to open our gate for him to even get a foothold.

A stronghold is defined as a "fortified city" with a great wall of resistance. As it applies to us being a three-part person, it is a mindset formed out of a belief system. Mindsets are often passed from one generation to the next. Satan uses them to veil, twist, and distort the truth of God. The lies become firmly planted in our minds as strongholds. The stronghold in the mind acts as the hub where our actions and sins originate. Everything starts in the heart, moves through the soul, and then to the flesh. Be alert and discerning to guard your inner court of the soul.

Like Parent, Like Child

You might have heard people say, "I didn't know any better, that was just the way I was raised." There is actually a lot of truth to that; we do think and act out of mindsets and belief systems according to how we were raised until we are old enough to 'get our own mind.' But if you have no drive or desire to be your own person searching for your individual identity, you will repeat this generational pattern.

It is common for a parent to raise their child to think a certain way; and that way is usually the way *they* were taught. A spirit of strife can easily become a part of the family dynamic when children begin to think for themselves and develop mindsets that differ from their parents' way of thinking. I believe this is why so many parents struggle with their teenagers, and even adult children. It is part of them finding their identity and getting a mind of their own; and when they are misunderstood or controlled, they will rebel. I know this to be true because I rebelled, and it was usually because I disagreed with my parents. I felt misunderstood but was trying to find my way and identity at the same time. I have found that with my own children, communication is key. My husband and I work hard to honor who God created them to be and do our best to communicate with them openly in regard to thoughts and beliefs. And there is always room for us to work on our communication skills.

For decades I did not know how to guard my thought life and operated under learned mindsets and value systems that allowed strongholds in my life. These mindsets didn't produce fruit but instead kept me bound. The most resistant one was my stronghold with food. I have since changed my mindset by the power of the Holy Spirit. He taught me to actively take thoughts captive and replace a faulty system with God's thoughts and truths. I practice making mindful and intentional decisions according to the Spirit's leading. The Holy Spirit restored me on all levels: spirit, mind, and body.

The most important place to begin this journey is in the spirit, the place where we originated by God's design. We are human, but the order of how we operate and think matters greatly. We are a spirit, we have a soul, and we live in a body.

THE ART OF FREEDOM

When we operate in this order in life, we create what I call The Art of Freedom Paradigm©. It's a spirit-soul-body cycle based on a belief system. It is crucial that when we deal with generational mindsets or learned behavior strongholds in our soul, we go right to the source and break the cycle in the spirit first. Once we recognize our detrimental ways, we can begin to come out of agreement with negative, toxic, or stagnant lifestyle choices and behaviors. This intentional thought choice, accompanied by prayer and the power of the Holy Spirit, will set you on the path to new and positive kingdom-identity behaviors and bring incredible freedom.

We are all in search of our identity and we desire to live out of that place with peace and purpose in our right mind. It is in our nature to want to know *who* we are and *whose* we are. There is an abundance of freedom in knowing our identity and the truth of whose we are. When we find it, then we can begin to know why we were born in the first place and fulfill our God-given destiny.

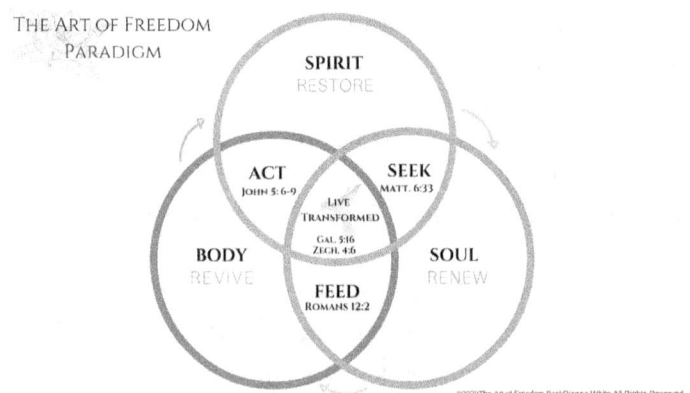

FREEDOM KEY

Be mindful and intentional of the order in which you operate. The Art of Freedom Paradigm© will produce peace and bring greater awareness of how to guard your heart and thought

THE ART OF GUARDING YOUR GATE

life. Stay entwined in the Vine and keep fellowship with the Holy Spirit.

Reflect and Record in Your Journal

Can you think of a time where you let down your guard and allowed the Enemy a foothold that caused havoc in your life? Do you expose your soul to the ways of the world by compromising your morals and standards? If so, why do you feel you have to do this? Is there a way that you can see yourself setting a new and better example for others? If so, explain what a typical situation might look like and how you could shift it in a better direction.

Prayer Empowerment

Heavenly Father, in the name of Jesus, I repent for not guarding my soul in greater ways. Holy Spirit teach me how to guard my gates only letting the things of you in. Please guard me against the things that I cannot control. Help me to have greater awareness of how I think and operate in life according to The Art of Freedom Paradigm©. Help me to think and seek first You, Your kingdom and righteousness. I repent if I have agreed to and operated under generational mindsets of learned behaviors not taking responsibility for myself. I choose to change that today! I want to be a curse breaker and change destiny for myself and my family or family to come. Thank you for removing these strongholds in my soul. I ask would become the stronghold over my soul from this day forward. Amen.

Chapter 15
THE ART OF NOT GOING BACK

No More Grave Mentality!

Graveclothes: The clothes or wrappings in which a body is buried, formally called cerements, are described as waxed cloth for wrapping a corpse.

My thoughts shifted to the Lord as I rolled out of bed. My schedule was open. It was going to be a casual day around the house with laundry, tidying up, writing, and a little painting. I put on sweatpants and the Lord said, "Get dressed." I thought, "I am getting dressed." He said, "No, get dressed in your real clothes."

I strolled to the closet and stared at my clothes. I said, "Okay Lord, what do you want me to wear?" I grabbed some nice jeans and a pair of shoes. I was undecided as to what top to wear. An old favorite caught my eye. I pulled the top over my head and it was now two sizes too big! I had lost so much weight that it just hung on me. It was worn out and needed to be retired. It had lost its original form. I felt frumpy and "undressed" but I was going to settle for the old shirt because of the comfort.

I heard the Lord ask, "Is that what you're going to wear?" I replied out loud, "Yes." He asked, "Why do you want to wear this shirt?" I told Him, "It's comfortable." He said, "Okay, wear it if you want but don't get too comfortable. Those are graveclothes!" I heard Him but didn't respond. He allowed me to finish dressing. As I slipped on my shoes, He continued to speak, "When you're finished getting dressed in what you've chosen, I want you to do your hair and makeup, too." I thought that was a bit extreme for a casual day around the house so I asked Him, "Lord, what are you preparing me for today?" He said, "This is who you are now. No longer do you wear graveclothes or a grave face. Present yourself as an excellent representative of Me. You are My Ambassador now! Be the best version of Me and let it begin in the heart and mind." Then He said, "Why would you want to wear old graveclothes that are comfortable when I've given you a new garment?"

Immediately I thought, "Oh, heck no!" and I ripped off the top and found a new garment in my closet faster than a Pentecostal could say "GLORY." I felt His love as I acknowledged my way of thinking and repented. He was teaching me Kingdom mentality.

I refuse to go back! I refuse to live alive in Him but remain bound in graveclothes. The graveclothes lifestyle starts in the mind. The Lord won't make our decisions for us; I had to decide. He proposed His way of thinking but left the choice to me. He suggested I get rid of some other worn-out clothes as well. I folded the old garment and piled up other garments that were part of the old me or brought back bad memories.

God cannot give us new blessings and transform us, nor can we operate in new supernatural thinking, if we still entertain and wear the old. We have to make room for the new. "Graveclothes" may be comfortable, but they don't help us become who He wants us to be. He already had a design in mind before He created us. He believes and still sees what we are supposed to be regardless of where we are in life. Staying in our carnal comfort zone keeps us from accomplishing the purpose He intended for us. We must crucify our fleshly desires and run in the opposite direction.

Say goodbye to that old grave mentality and thinking that life is supposed to be "comfortable." We will never accomplish anything of eternal value by living from a comfortable place. The only thing that grows in comfort is our seat. Our flesh is a spiritual growth inhibitor that will take us in the opposite direction of Kingdom principles. The Word of God says the desire alone to do good is not enough to overcome our flesh. We must hide God's Word in our hearts and be empowered by the Holy Spirit to avoid the lusts of the flesh. Our desire to obey the Lord grows as out of our love for Him.

"I have hidden your word in my heart that I might not sin against you" (Psalm 119:11, NIV).

Apostle Paul adds detail in Galatians 5:16-18: "But I say, walk by the Spirit, and you will not carry out the desire of the flesh. For the flesh sets its desire against the Spirit, and the Spirit against the flesh; for these are in opposition to one another, so that you may not do the things that you please. But if you are led by the Spirit, you are not under the Law." (NASB Bible.com)

What is it that the Lord is trying to get you to get rid of that resembles your old life or graveclothes? Examine your spiritual, physical, and mental life, and ask the Lord what it is that needs to go so you can become the best possible version of you. Look in the mirror and ask Him to show you if there are any signs of the grave present. It's time to put your faith to work and seek Him for help and guidance.

For you were bought at a price; therefore, glorify God in your body and in your spirit, which are God's.

—1 Corinthians 6:20, NKJV

Freedom Key

Take spiritual, mental, emotional, and physical inventory of yourself and possessions that may be growth inhibitors. Let go of all things that represent "graveclothes."

Prayer Empowerment

Holy Spirit help me to value myself as a new creation and God's holy temple. Remind me daily of who I am in You and that I deserve nothing less than the best from You in spirit, soul, body, and possessions. Remind me that nothing grows in places of comfort and help me to resist complacency. Jesus, I receive all that You died to give me by coming out of the grave and ascending into heaven. Today I choose to not to go back! Fill me with Your fire and give me a passion to live each day with purpose for You—no more graveclothes or grave face—in the name of Jesus, Amen.

PART FOUR

The Art of Reviving the Body:
Let Your Kingdom Come in Me

Chapter 16
The Art of Reviving the Body

Our Bodies Are Not Our Own

Don't you realize that your body is the temple of the Holy Spirit, who lives in you and was given to you by God? You do not belong to yourself.

—1 Corinthians 6:19, NLT

We live most of our lives in a reactive state to situations or circumstances when truly we should be living from a proactive or preventive state. We make our bodies and practices into idols and call it free will. It is free will but not when we have made a commitment to serve a holy God. When we receive the Holy Spirit of Christ and renounce and turn from our sinful ways, we are no longer ours, we have new hearts and our bodies now house a Holy God.

When I received the diagnosis of fibromyalgia, I was driven to find a solution and began my own search for health alternatives. Until that point, I lived a carnally minded life even though I'd been born again in the Spirit for years. This lifestyle of a new heart, but satisfying the flesh, was not serving me well.

I believed the doctor who said there was hope and began to search for solutions. A fibromyalgia cookbook helped me understand that the things I put into my mouth affected me greatly. The dietary neglect, along with my toxic thought life and negative self-talk, was a recipe for disaster. Even though my problem did not entirely start with food, food was complicating and aiding my sickness, both emotionally and physically. I learned about white refined sugar, white processed flours, aspartame, and more. It was an eye opener for me when I realized that I had control over what I was allowing to intrude, invade, and occupy my body. I was sabotaging myself!

Our bodies are considered a terrain and, when not taken care of well, will react and produce pain and detrimental health conditions. I was affected by the story and teachings of Jordan Rubin, a biblical health coach, and author of multiple books, including *The Maker's Diet*. I learned about digestive health and the importance of taking probiotics and digestive enzymes. Until this point the only health supplement I had ever taken was vitamin C or a multivitamin.

Rubin's book, *The Maker's Diet*, included a before and after picture of him. I saw an emaciated man dying from a digestive disease and then saw him restored to complete health. I had seen people's bodies be transformed by losing drastic amounts of weight but I had never seen anyone restored to health and transformed like he had been! As time went on, I looked at the picture to remind me that I, too, could be healed and made healthy again. This is proof of the power of vision for good. Vision once again gave me hope.

He had been healed and restored by God through prayer, knowledge and application of the Holy Scriptures, diet and lifestyle changes. I realized that I truly was perishing from lack of knowledge. I began to take one little step at a time, following the fibromyalgia cookbook and Rubin's biblical health teachings. I cleaned up my eating and I made lifestyle changes. I incorporated digestive health supplements and other life-giving supplements like chelated organic magnesium, olive leaf extract, and vitamins B and D from a company called To Your Health. The most beneficial one I found through them was Fibro-Care©. My friend Dianne, a local florist who suffered from fibromyalgia and chronic fatigue symptoms, suggested the product. She said it saved her life and enabled her to run her business.

Fibro-Care© is loaded with pure chelated magnesium, malic acid, B and C vitamins, and manganese. She gave me my first bottle and encouraged me to pay it forward one day. I still use To Your Health products and have paid it forward many times by giving others their first bottle. To learn more about these products go to www.e-tyh.com.

I was overwhelmed with all the new information and changes I had to make but I still had peace that this was the right way. These new adjustments seemed to help me improve from my state of chronic fatigue but only for short periods. I still had to deal with the root issues deep inside. The changes I made provided relief, but I was still suffering from low self-worth. I still had an imperfect perspective of myself that hindered my healing and put me right back into a cycle of defeat. Although I was adamant about my healing and continually in prayer, the defeated mentality would send me right back to eating poorly. The doctors continued to be stumped at my condition and would change my prescriptions or up the dosage. The medications were counteracting what I was trying to do in my body and spirit. The veil had not yet been lifted for me to truly see; but I was on my way.

Like Rubin, traditional medicine provided no answers for me; it only complicated things. I was determined to find a solution. I had to ask myself, "What am I feeding my spirit, soul, and body?" It was clear that I had to make more changes and ask Holy Spirit to help me. There were no shortcuts for good long-term health. The more I learned about digestive health, implemented Rubin's teachings, and took his supplements, the better I felt. But much work—the deep work—still had to be done. No diet plan, not even a healthy one, was going to change me and sustain me until I dealt with my heart and soul issues. I continued striving to adapt to this new way of eating and thinking.

Apostle Paul teaches us, "All things are lawful for me, but not all things are helpful; all things are lawful for me, but not all things edify. Let no one seek his own, but each one the other's well-being" (1 Corinthians 10:23-24, NKJV).

I had to become dedicated to this new lifestyle and would get frustrated that I was not seeing instant results, but I kept believing. Regardless of my belief, I was trying to do it through my own strength and understanding, so the results took longer. I believe we are called not to lean on our own understanding but to acknowledge Him in all ways; but I was only acknowledging Him on an as-needed basis, and I reaped what I sowed.

The Importance of Fasting

It's not about what you're giving up, it's about what you're gaining: "It is written, man shall not live by bread alone, but by every word that proceeds from the mouth of God" (Matthew 4:4, NKJV).

It was evident that my body was in a state of inflammation beyond repair by medication. I had learned of gut health and the importance of a raw and whole-foods diet from *The Maker's Diet,* but I didn't understand the extent of the source of the inflammation. I saw a new doctor who put me on a blend of omegas and advised me to get the book *The Daniel Fast.* She wanted me to follow it for twenty-one days! I thought I was going to die. The only liquid allowed on the diet was water and there were no meats or sweets. I could eat whole grains, vegetables, and beans. This wasn't just a diet; for me it was torture. It was then that I realized that my dependency on food for comfort and security had become an idol. This was a turning point in my pursuit of health and freedom. This catapulted me and my body into a forced fast.

A fast should be prompted and commissioned by the Holy Spirit for it to accomplish its purpose. The Holy Spirit provides the power to endure the fast and breaks strongholds that nothing else can. After Jesus was baptized in the water by John, the Holy Spirit descended upon Him like a dove and He was filled and empowered by the Holy Spirit. Immediately following His baptism, the Spirit led Him to the wilderness to be tested and he fasted for forty days and forty nights, while angels ministered to Him. This leads me to believe that, when led by the Spirit, we can fast successfully, empowered with a grace from God. I completed the fast and felt better. Fasting still offers spiritual and physical benefits for us today.

As I sought the Holy Spirit for continual help, He gave me strength to apply the health teachings I had learned, and I would fast. He destroyed my idol of food, breaking the strongholds I had in my soul. Death was literally losing! When I began to feel weak and tempted, He would remind me, "Fasting is the way to starve what needs to die and feed what needs to thrive!" This reminder was all I needed to press on and not give in. I knew I no longer had to fight this battle on my own. I felt empowered!

Let Your Kingdom Come in Me

The Holy Spirit gave me supernatural strength to persevere and it became easier and easier to resist and say "no." I took small steps and tracked my progress. I cut my portions in half. I asked for a to-go box when dining out. I cut back drastically on my sugar and bread. I gave up fried foods. I replaced the bad fats with good fats like avocado, salmon, extra virgin olive oil, whole eggs, nuts, chia seeds, dark chocolate (over 70% cocoa), coconut, and coconut oil. The cravings for unhealthy food began to diminish rapidly, my taste buds began to change, and it got easier over time. This was a quick work of the Lord for sure, but it was still a process.

I set goals and recorded my wins in my journal. I rejoiced with God in the pages of my journal with words of gratitude for His faithfulness. When I met my goals, I rewarded myself with something other than food. This season of my life initiated a supernatural acceleration of weight loss. With my hunger being more for God than for food, the fasting became easier and my zeal for life returned. I put into place simple and achievable exercise activities like gentle meditative stretching and walking. I increased my distance as I gained strength and stamina. The exercise was great for my body, as well as my mental clarity and peace of mind. Eventually this place of physical engagement became a secret place where the Lord would speak to me. The other habits I put into practice included:

- Drink sixteen ounces of purified water first thing in the morning with a super greens blend.

- Start the day with a smoothie made of unsweetened almond milk, raw organic plant protein products, chia seeds, milled flax seed, fresh kale or spinach, fresh or frozen fruit, or a bowl of unsweetened plain organic Greek yogurt with organic granola, using raw local honey in place of sugar for smoothies or yogurt. Choose low glycemic berries and fruit; use one-third or one-half of a banana in smoothies.

- In winter start the day with organic unsweetened oatmeal, honey, fruit, and nuts.

- Take water everywhere and drink at least eight ounces before the largest meal.

- Keep low to medium glycemic snacks on hand, like an apple, healthy protein bar, or pack of trail mix.

- Stop eating out of bags and boxes, and portion food.

- Use and carry liquid stevia sweetener. Use absolutely no aspartame or other artificial sweeteners—diet sodas and sugar-free items, including gum, are loaded with them.

- Split restaurant meals and desserts two to three ways; no second helpings at home or buffets. Limit visiting restaurants that are a temptation. Take an alternate route to your destination if you are tempted by particular places.

- No eating after 7 p.m.

- Incorporate intermittent fasting regularly (for example, an eight-hour eating window between 11 a.m. and 7 p.m.)

- Take twenty to thirty-minute walks 3x a week or break it into five to ten-minute walks several times a week as a great way to start back into activity and build up stamina without being overwhelmed. Wear your normal clothes. The point is to get out of the house and move. You will soon be able to walk farther and longer.

The Holy Spirit was empowering me, and the discipline and fruit of self-control was active in my life. My submission to the Holy Spirit and small acts of obedience reaped great rewards for my body and self-esteem. God cares about our self-esteem. He wants us to take pride in the person He created us to be, proud of ourselves and the work He has done in us. We are His children and should feel proud of our achievements and allow it to empower us to help inspire and change the world around us. By doing this it brings glory to Him. Anyone can put these practices into place. If I can do it, I truly believe you can do it, too!

The key to a successful relationship with food lies in our hearts, our identity in Christ, and our fellowship with Holy Spirit. We can be empowered to conquer this area once and for all if we get to the root of the issue and break generational patterns and strongholds. I firmly believe God wants you healed, whole, and healthy in all ways. We must seek God's perspective. God is not glorified in our brokenness until we let Him in to mend it. We must first realize our relationship with food goes much deeper than our stomachs. He wants to deal with our health so we can be all He created us to be.

I was working out The Art of Freedom Paradigm© in my own life by seeking Him first and caring for my spirit and soul, but also taking physical action. This would eventually turn into the spirit-soul-body point of convergence and result in total transformation. The people and products that I embraced in this season were another watering of that original seed of hope on my road to healing and wholeness.

It's time to get back to the basics to see what God says about food, health, and the supplements He created to help us live well and thrive co-laboring with the Holy Spirit. I am confident that God can heal your body just as He did for me.

Freedom Key

Educate yourself, be mindful of what you eat, and incorporate intermittent fasting and light to moderate physical activity. When you feel tempted or weak, seek and ask Holy Spirit for help. Spend ample time in prayer, worship, reading the word of God and fellowship with Holy Spirit during times of fasting.

Reflect and Record in Your Journal

What is your relationship with food? Are there any areas that you need to surrender to the Lord? Is there an unhealthy pattern and connection between your eating habits and emotions?

Record your answers and ask Holy Spirit to help you submit and surrender these areas to Him to increase your fruit of self-control and heal the original root of the stronghold.

Prayer Empowerment

Heavenly Father, in the name of Jesus, I need you to help me with my unhealthy relationship with food and toxic thinking regarding my physical health. I repent for making food an idol. I receive your forgiveness and ask you Holy Spirit to guide me and strengthen me in this journey to make wise and healthy decisions for my physical health. I repent for neglecting my body and for not seeking greater knowledge to take care of myself, your holy temple. Lord, please break all strongholds that may have become toxic patterns from generational habits and cultural practices. As I bravely walk away from my food and drink idols and move forward in this journey please empower me to resist temptation. Increase my hunger for you God, instead of filling myself with food and drink. Let Your kingdom come in me. All glory to You. Amen.

Chapter 17
The Art of Rest

Operating from the Green Pasture

He makes me lie down in green pastures; He leads me beside still waters. He restores my soul.

—Psalm 23, NKJV

Let's be honest, who really lies down in a green pasture or sits by still waters to be restored? It seems that society has taught us that rest, retreat, and recreation are for the rich and famous. This couldn't be further from the truth. God designed our bodies to need all these things and for good reason. He knew that each of these activities—along with clean living, eating, and digesting His Word—would restore us over and over again. After all, He rested and Jesus retreated, often! After each day of creation God sat back, reflected, rested, and saw that it was good. Jesus would often retreat away from crowds to spend time being restored in the Father's presence. The LORD gave us the perfect example of how to operate from rest. He gave us the rhythms and seasons of creation. That rhythm goes like this: rise with Him, work with Him, reflect with Him, and rest with Him. In addition to this perfect example, He gave us seasons. In the Bible, the sons of Issachar knew and understood the signs of the times and seasons. Their ability to know and understand the times was a gift of wisdom and discernment in order for Israel to know what to do (1 Chronicles 12:32, NKJV). This was divine strategy!

The demands we choose and say "yes" to in our life do not allow for ample time to reflect, rest, or retreat. We think of rest simply as physically sitting still when it has a much deeper meaning in its original context. The word "rest" actually has many meanings. The first definition according to the Bible comes from the Hebrew word *nuach*, meaning to rest, to be quiet. Sometimes, it is synonymous with *shabat*: to cease, stop, or rest. The Greek word *anapausis* means cessation and refreshment. I particularly like the word meaning refreshment! God built in refreshment for our lives every day and even gave us permission to take a whole day for refreshing. That is a refreshing thought!

The second meaning comes with a layer of greater spiritual understanding that can aid our physical action and mental state. Rest ultimately means to trust in a secure source. Nothing challenges me more than trust! This is where our faith of a mustard seed steps in and is tested. Trust is an action to our faith. The Bible says "knowing that the testing of your faith (and trust) produces patience" (James 1:3, NKJV).

Christ's rest is not a rest *from* work, but *in* work; yes, in work! God created us to work and it is a good thing for our spirit, mind, and body! Jesus was secure and trusted His source. When was the last time you rested in work with a trust and security in your source? Jesus rested in the harmonious working of all the faculties and affections of will, heart, imagination, and conscience because each had found in God the ideal sphere of its satisfaction and development (Vine's Concise Dictionary). He modeled the art of rest perfectly as a whole person!

This is how I can rest while painting, writing, teaching, or mentoring; and from it I am restored on many levels. I feel alive, revived, and satisfied. Even though I am working, I am resting in my work in His presence, harmoniously in cooperation with Holy Spirit. There is a sweet reward that comes from trust that allows us to enter the Lord's rest; whether that is in our spirit, soul, or body. If we are not fully trusting, then we cannot fully rest.

I know that when reading the Bible, it's hard to picture ourselves as the character in the story; but this truly was an example given to us by David in order to be revived, restored, refreshed, strengthened, and equipped. Yes, even equipped! The Lord took a shepherd boy and turned him into a warrior (1 Samuel 17, NKJV).

David was the youngest of eight. In biblical numerology, eight was a symbol of resurrection and regeneration, aligning with a new beginning. Even though David was the youngest and not chosen to be sent into battle, he was the one most confident and equipped to defeat the giant. He spent his day in the pasture shepherding his father's flocks. He obeyed the commands of his father Jesse even when he was asked to take bread to the front lines. As a boy who often fought bears and lions to protect the flock, David was already a warrior at heart. I like to think that he was excited to see some action at the front lines but was sorely disappointed in his brothers, who hid as cowards. How was young David so confident that he could take on a towering and beastly man? He was sent to the front lines for such a time as this, but he could not have confronted the giant if he had not regularly been spending time in the pasture with his Heavenly Father. While he tended to his earthly father's business, he talked to God, meditated on His word, played and sang songs to the LORD, and became strong in his spirit, soul, and body. Just like Jesus, David rested in the harmonious workings of all the faculties and affections of will, heart, imagination, and conscience, and in the source of his strength. David was so confident of his God because he knew Him. David was not threatened by this giant and he was not going to let a beast of a man mock him or his God. David was equipped for battle in his secret place.

This is a perfect example of finding rest in the work we do in partnership with the LORD, while we are being restored, revived, refreshed, strengthened, and equipped to fight our battles. Apart from finding rest in what we do, we need to cease from working on a regular basis to rest our bodies; but often we don't enter into the Lord's rest where we are truly refreshed.

We Need the Lord's Strategy

Before many breakthroughs in the Bible, the Lord would command his troops to first set up camp and scout the lay of the land, seeking a strategy before charging the enemy. Before Joshua led the Israelites to the promised land across the Jordan River, he was commanded to camp for three days by the river's bank. The Israelites waited on Joshua to give the command and lead them across. He commanded them to sanctify themselves because they were going to follow the sacred ark of the covenant of the LORD on dry ground and they needed to be pure to enter the promised land. It was holy ground, where the presence of the LORD passed through and where He was taking them. If Joshua had not sought the Lord and waited to receive His orders and His strategy, it might have been a fatal disaster.

This is an important part of understanding the strategy of rest. We must seek God first for a strategy on how to fight our battles. In my case, that meant sitting with Him daily in my secret place, worshiping, fasting, painting, writing, walking, meeting with life-giving friends, and taking an occasional day or more away from earthly demands. It was in these places that I was able to be refreshed and revived through work, physical rest, physical and mental discipline, and recreation, resulting in a restored state of spirit, soul, and body. I would feel revived when I left these places even if it was work. It felt amazing that I didn't have to escape life anymore. I was enjoying life and wanted to be alive. I stopped running and I learned to enter in the Lord's rest. I was learning the perfect *art of rest* from the rhythm of creation that God intended for us to follow.

This strategy only comes by one way: the way of wisdom that is the mind of God. Holy Spirit is the giver of wisdom and explains what to expect when we seek it.

> [1]My son, if you receive my words, And treasure my commands within you,
>
> [2]So that you incline your ear to wisdom, And apply your heart to understanding;
>
> [3]Yes, if you cry out for discernment, And lift up your voice for understanding,
>
> [4]If you seek her as silver, And search for her as for hidden treasures;
>
> [5]Then you will understand the fear of the Lord, And find the knowledge of God.
>
> [6]For the Lord gives wisdom; From His mouth come knowledge and understanding;
>
> —Proverbs 2:1-6 NKJV

The use of our gifts without the wisdom of God can be reckless and ineffective. The LORD equipped his craftsman Bezalel with wisdom to build the temple in the middle of the wilderness. He filled him with wisdom and knowledge, and equipped him with skill to carry out the building process according to God's blueprints.

> See, I have called by name Bezalel the son of Uri, the son of Hur, of the tribe of Judah. And I have filled him with the Spirit of God, in wisdom, in understanding, in knowledge, and in all manner of workmanship, to design artistic works, to work in gold, bronze, in cutting jewels for setting, in carving wood, and to work in all manner of workmanship.
>
> —Exodus 31:2, NKJV

Everything in the temple—from the menorah to the ark of the covenant and even the anointing oil—all was created by the wisdom and knowledge of God. Our gifts are vehicles for our assignment. We have to know the One who gives us our assignment and allow the Holy Spirit to navigate our path for our gifts to accomplish God's purpose effectively.

Your Gift Is a Weapon

> For the weapons of our warfare are not carnal but mighty in God for pulling down strongholds, casting down arguments and every high thing that exalts itself against the knowledge of God, bringing every thought captive to the obedience of Christ, and being ready to punish all disobedience when your obedience is fulfilled.
>
> —2 Corinthians 10:3-6, NKJV

As I learned to rest and retreat to my studio several times a week, I realized that it was in this place that I wasn't just painting, I was also praying. One day I noticed a shift in my studio time. I became hyper-focused and very serious about what I was painting. I began to flow in my intuitive gift. I would listen to worship music; the Holy Spirit would come over me, and I would stop praying or singing and begin to paint rapidly. I was working in my gift of intercession through painting. Whatever Holy Spirit was moving me to feel was what needed to be released in the spirit realm when I was painting. I would hear key phrases or scriptures and begin to pray as I painted and believed the kingdom keys would be released.

I have found my creative gift to be of good use in my battle to keep mental clarity. There is a continual war over our soul. The enemy can't take our salvation, but he can set up camp in our soul if we allow him. I described this in chapter fourteen on guarding our gate. John 1:13 makes it clear that those who belong to God are not born again by their own will, but by God's will. It is only by the Holy Spirit that we are drawn to salvation. This is why the battle is always over our mind. It is the middle ground of our being. We cannot give the devil space there. But sometimes I find unnecessary chatter in the heavenly realms that begin to block thoughts and creative streams. This comes as no surprise because Satan was originally the most gifted, beautiful angel and minister of music until he and other fallen angels were kicked out of heaven for desiring to be worshiped as god. The spirit of pride plucked him out of heaven.

Have you ever thought of the struggle of the creative ones? Maybe that's you. Ask anyone on the outside and they will probably tell you that being an artist, musician, dancer, author, or poet is a romantic hobby. Only a lucky few, such as Ernest Hemmingway, become masters and legends. Hemingway, a war veteran, had a gift to write novels. Regardless of the riches, his life resulted in struggle. There was a battle over his brilliant mind. There is a multitude of artists on the earth and the Lord wants to redeem the creative sphere for His Kingdom and His glory. Satan has distorted, twisted, and perverted art on the earth since the beginning of time. The further along we get in the last days, it seems that creative expressions get gorier, more perverted, and downright disgusting, and have nothing to do with our "good, good Father." I am confident this is the reason that believing or unbelieving artists fight such a hard battle of identity and success in who they are and what they do. We creative people have been given an incredible voice but what we choose to say with that voice is where the problems lie. Satan does not want us to have the privilege of co-creating with the Father because he no longer can. This is why he attacks creative souls so fiercely.

God is reclaiming this area for Himself and it is happening at an accelerated rate right now on the earth. He is raising up and calling out creative people who know Him, know His word, understand the calling, and are walking an upright life with Him through Holy Spirit.

Do Not Forsake Your Secret Place

When I step away from painting for any period of time, I begin to feel a void and don't fully experience peace of mind. At one point during the writing of this book, I hit a mental roadblock. I was overwhelmed, mentally tired, and my creative thought stream seemed to have stopped. There was junk clogging up my Holy Spirit funnel. I closed the laptop and walked away, frustrated. I spoke to my friend Wendy and was sharing my struggle and frustration with her. I told her how I had missed painting and realized it had been a month since I had picked up my brushes. She encouraged me to take time to paint. I went to bed that night with the intention of taking a break from the book and returning to painting.

That night I dreamed I was sitting in a beautiful green pasture on a quilt next to a man seated on my right. It was understood that I was there to enjoy the view, fellowship, and rest; but I was also there to study the field and flowers in order to paint them. At first, the man in my dream vaguely resembled my earthly father in his younger days; but it was clear in my spirit that it was Father God. As I looked around behind me there was a still body of water, like a small lake. In front of me was a wide open dusty green field with tiny blue flowers, periwinkle in color. In the distance in front of me there was a u-shaped border around the pasture with tall trees that looked like columns, and around them were big flowers that looked like birds of paradise and artichokes. They were a mix of dusty green, periwinkle, and teal. They wrapped up and around the columns on a vine. The trees went as high as I could see. The colors were vibrant, and the atmosphere was serene. I was awed by how beautiful and peaceful it was.

I glanced down to my left and noticed there were two broken-stemmed flowers lying near me. They looked like they had just been tossed aside and were lying on the grass. The man sitting to my right got up and went into the field. I was taking in the view and experiencing it on an emotional level so I could paint it. Just when I was about to paint, the man came walking towards me; but this time I could see only his body in an ivory cloak. As his hand extended towards me, he said, "Don't forget your flowers," and he tossed the two broken-stemmed flowers onto my paper in front of me. They were deep purple in color. The Spirit began to minister to me at this point and said, "Do not forget to come to the secret place often to fellowship and paint. We meet with you when you are operating in your gifts; it is where you receive directly from the Father's hand. It is where you receive the orders for your assignments." I agreed and gladly received the instruction. He reminded me to be not just a spectator of the sights, but a participator. Those were *my* flowers *He* was giving me to paint. I had a responsibility to both the flowers and Him.

That morning I called my friend Wendy and I was so excited to share my dream with her. She was rejoicing with me and reminded me of a vision she had gotten for me in prayer a short time earlier. She said, "Dionne, don't you remember the vision I received when I was in prayer for you? Do you remember? I saw a painting with the little blue flowers!" I remembered immediately but it had slipped my mind while I was writing this book and in a mental fog. I thanked God for

Wendy and her obedience. My heart was filled with gratitude towards Him for his love and faithfulness to pursue me on this matter.

Later that day, I took time to paint and I could feel the stress melt away, the mental fog lift, and the creativity flow again. I heard the Holy Spirit say, "You can't do one without the other." I knew exactly what He meant. He was telling me that in order to write, I had to paint; in order to do anything within my calling and assignments, I had to paint. In no time the atmospheric chatter was silenced, the static was cleared, and the block was removed. I learned a valuable lesson to not forsake my secret places.

The next morning Holy Spirit reminded me of young David again in the green pasture, how his time there prepared him, and how his gift became a weapon for good in time of need. His music could chase away tormenting spirits and his courage defeated a giant.

Our gift of creating can be a spiritual weapon. When we meet with God in the green pasture, we receive inspiration, revelation, instruction, and motivation to fight the giants in life. We can use our gift to release the heart of the Father in the earth. As we discussed earlier, the word of God is living, active, and sharper than any two-edged sword. When I was painting in and with Holy Spirit, that living and active word was being distributed into my work to go forth and accomplish its purpose. Our creative gift has been given to us to be used as a calling for the purposes of God. He desires you to use your gift not only as a hobby for personal gain but to change destinies and shift atmospheres.

If David had not spent time in his secret place working with the LORD, ministering to the LORD, and cultivating His gifts, he would not have been equipped to go into battle and defeat Goliath. The purpose behind God's design of the green pasture was so we could reap the benefits of it. I don't consider my time in rest, retreat, recreation, or relaxation to be an act of procrastination; rather, it is learning to practice His presence in everyday life. Leonardo da Vinci was a master at many creative expressions in addition to painting, and he knew the importance of rest. I believe he was a genius because he learned the art of rest and retreat.

When he was painting "The Last Supper" in the church of Santa Maria delle Grazie in Milan, Leonardo spent many hours in apparent idleness out in the cloister, much to the annoyance of the monks who were paying for his services. Eventually, a delegation went to the artist and complained that the church was not getting its money's worth. Leonardo heard them out, then explained simply, "When I pause the longest, I make the most telling strokes with my brush."

Leonardo goes on to encourage us, "Every now and then, go away, take a little relaxation, because when you come back to your work, your judgment will be surer. To remain constantly at work will cause you to lose the power of judgment. Go some distance away from it, because then the work appears smaller and more of it can be taken in at a glance, and a lack of harmony or proportion is more readily seen" (Ray Ashford, "A lesson in effectiveness" from *The Quiet Life*).

We receive ideas, inspiration, fresh perspective, and power when we rest and retreat in the Lord. I believe Leonardo da Vinci was filling his creative well and seeking direction for the next stroke or next invention.

Along with painting, my walks have become a place of mental and spiritual clarity filling my creative well. One evening on a walk, I approached the local community flower garden. It is kept up by a precious lady in our neighborhood. I stopped and greeted her as she was tending the garden. It was in full bloom and brimming with vibrant reds, oranges, yellows, pinks, and purples. I began to take photos for study, and I heard the Lord say, "If you don't walk to see the flowers then how are you supposed to paint them? Most people are too busy and drive everywhere in a hurry and never truly get to see the flowers. That is why I have called you to paint them." I felt so important in that moment. God had given me a task: to paint *His* flowers. He was basically saying that we need to stop and smell the roses or at least slow down to see them.

He was right, if I don't step out of the house to see, feel, and smell the reality of flowers then I won't really know them. And if I don't know them I can't paint them. More importantly, if I don't know Him, I can't paint His message. I'm not out to make my point or paint my message. I am His artist and I will paint and write whatever He asks me to.

It is important that we do a routine examination of our state of rest. The way of the world tells us to chase after money and work, work, work in our own strength; but we only end up burned out and wanting to escape life. If we do not have a foundation and identity in Christ, we will never be satisfied with any amount of money, work, or rest. Your purpose now is to release His truth, light, and love, displaying His glory so that all mankind might be drawn to Him.

There is a rhythm to this rest. Imagine the ocean. The rhythm of rest is an ebb and flow experience where the water is the carrier and you are on a board following the wave, riding the surf. Holy Spirit is that water and the board is your life, and you have to partner with Him to maintain your balance by being centered on that board or you will wipe out. If our feet are not firm on the board and our eyes aren't looking ahead, the surf will throw us every time. We have to trust Him and know Him personally by studying the word of God and spending time in His presence. We need to learn of His rhythms and know when to ease up and when to turn; but we are still resting and trusting Him. It is all part of entering the rest of the Lord.

Are you finding rest and purpose in what you are doing? He is pursuing you this very moment and there is always an open invitation to be with, and create with, Him. Can you hear His whisper to come away with Him?

Freedom Key

Do not forsake the secret place or green pasture.

Reflect and Record in Your Journal

When was the last time you truly felt at rest? What were you doing? In what area do you feel you need to rest and trust more? What does your secret place(s) practice look like? Can you see your gift as a weapon for good when used in partnership with the Lord? Have you already experienced a spiritual breakthrough by using your creative gifts? Explain.

Ask God to help you surrender these areas to Him and engage with the Holy Spirit, asking Him to help train your "hands" for war as you rest and co-labor with Him.

Prayer Empowerment

Heavenly Father, in the name of Jesus, thank you for the gift of rest. Jesus, thank you for modeling the art of rest and showing us how we can live, work, and play daily as we enter into your rest by trusting you. I repent for not resting, retreating and trusting you enough. Lord, help me to thrive and no longer hustle and strive with selfish ambition. I am asking for Your strategy so you can raise me to be a warrior for you. Show me how to abide in your rest so that I can use it and my gift as a weapon for the kingdom of God and a be blessing to the world. Holy Spirit pursue me daily and help me not to forsake the secret places. I will choose to rise with you, work with you, reflect with you, and rest with you. Holy Spirit teach me the rhythm of rest daily to be more than a conqueror in all areas of my life for Your glory. Amen.

Chapter 18
The Art of Painting the Promise

Healing and Wholeness through Creative Spiritual Transformation

The LORD's promises are pure, like silver refined in a furnace, purified seven times over.

—Psalm 12:6, NLT

Being a kingdom painter, writer, prophet and teacher, my responsibility is to release into the earth what God speaks to me. When I do that in spirit and truth, the avenue of the art carries a living and active message. Co-creating is a form of worship and a responsibility that we are privileged to share in. We are called to respond to the Spirit. If you have the ability and revelation of this truth, then it becomes your responsibility as a child of God. I find when I spend ample time in worship, thanking and adoring God— singing of His goodness first— my works and words have an energy behind them that is not of me. Matthew 6:33 offers a promise, "But seek first His kingdom and His righteousness and all these things will be added." Often, while I engage in worship the Holy Spirit prepares me to paint, write or speak. I begin to feel a tug on my heart and mind that may lead to the canvas or the computer. This is why a time of worship matters in our everyday lives; it primes and directs us for the day, resulting in kingdom work (Proverbs 3:5-6).

After a time of worship, I head to my easel while I can feel and see the message that needs to come forth. Up, down, around, back and forth the brush goes. It is as if time flies and stands still at the same time. The result from the previous time of worship produces a living, active painting that carries a message of hope, peace, power, joy, and healing or all of them.

When this happens, I am operating in both a divine and psychological flow. It is a type of convergence that allows us to create on a natural level that which has been fueled and infused by a supernatural force from Holy Spirit. Mihaly Csikszentmihalyi (pronounced me-high cheek-sent-me-high) is a Hungarian-American psychologist. He recognized and named the psychological concept of *flow* as a highly focused mental state.

Mihaly says, "Flow is being completely involved in an activity for its own sake. The ego falls away. Time flies. Every action, movement, and thought follow inevitably from the previous one, like playing jazz."

This state of flow does not apply just to painting or music, it can apply to any creative or repetitive activity. I propose that flow in the Spirit, driven by worship, ***is more than*** just doing something repetitive or therapeutic that only results in psychological effects. When you are doing something repetitive, it calms the brain and brings you to a relaxed state. This is why creative arts and hobbies are therapeutic and cause you to feel happy. Going one step beyond that is when you begin to engage the creative side in the Spirit, focusing and setting your mind on things above (Colossians 3:3), communicating with the Spirit, enjoying what you are doing, reaping healthy results and releasing kingdom impact. When done without the Spirit's engagement, you may only experience catharsis on a psychological and soul level; and this has to be maintained from the place of our soul. Catharsis is the release of tension and anxiety that results from bringing repressed feelings, and possibly traumatic memories, into consciousness. When this is done apart from the ministry of the Holy Spirit it can be damaging or even delay a person's healing and recovery. Many find temporary relief but have to seek counseling or therapy for a lifetime or return to that task every time the trauma is triggered. This is because they are not healing the trauma, they are only escaping it or learning to manage it.

Worship and creative practice are a gateway to the divine intersection of heaven and earth meant to produce heavenly results on earth. It is easier to get into flow quickly when we prime our time with intentional worship. Otherwise, when we put our hand to our task it could be an hour before we are working in divine or psychological flow. The reason it takes so long without the interaction and engagement of Holy Spirit is because we are literally taking the time to teach our soul what it needs to do and give our brain time to respond. Simply said, soul work delays spiritual transformation.

After I began experiencing creativity through worship and flow, I noticed other things in my life began to change in an accelerated way. God used my gift of painting to heal me and show me my worth again. He showed me that I needed to share my gift with the world. I began to find fulfillment and purpose. He gave each of us gifts and talents primarily because our gifts and talents connect us to Him. Secondly, He enables us to bless others with our gift.

My studio is one of the secret places for me to connect, hear, and arm myself with truth from a place of love. God used my time with Him in these secret places to deliver me from depression, anxiety, and lack of self-worth. Brushstroke after brushstroke, I immersed myself in His love and truth and He reached deep inside me to show me the promise.

He would heal past hurts and distorted perspectives, reveal and chase away lies, and replace them with truth! It was then that I coined the phrase "Painting the Promise" and began to create what I now teach as Creative Spiritual Transformation©. This concept of creativity as a means of healing that results in transformation has proven itself to me and others I've taught. It is a lifeline. I have been given a gift to help others blaze their own path to peace through worship and understanding spiritual flow with creativity as the avenue.

As I began studying art as a hobby and a means of therapy and healing, I noticed a pattern in the available curriculums. There was a definite distinction between what we might call secular and Christian programs. But there was not an overlapping or blending of them. The Lord prodded me to remedy this and led me to design a creative curriculum based on biblical principles that include Holy Spirit, psychological, and practical applications. His desire was that people would encounter Him, activate and renew their minds, and experience the expression of creativity with Holy Spirit. There needed to be a curriculum that would incorporate both the secular and the sacred. The concept of Creative Spiritual Transformation© that I have experienced and developed includes all three: spirit, soul, and body.

Some programs I looked into and studied were based solely on psychology, some were only spiritual, and some were designed simply for self-help and relaxation through practical application. I was not seeing a balanced program for all three. God created our spirits, our soul, psyche, and our bodies; so, I saw a need to engage all three. With His help, I created The A.C.T. Series~ The Awake. Create. Transform Curriculum©. The curriculum is based on Biblical principles and allows us to engage spiritually, mentally, emotionally, and in practical application through creative expression, resulting in a revived being of purpose. Practicing creative expression is a necessity for whole-person wellbeing. The first volume in the series—A.C.T. ONE: *Awake*, focuses on developing your identity as an artist and helping you connect with God on greater levels as you begin to engage your sanctified imagination. The curriculum is designed to help participants grow spiritually, intellectually, and creatively.

Painting started out as a teenage hobby and became a place of retreat as I began to experience the storms of life and the cruelty of the world. Three decades later, it is necessary to my wellbeing, especially my mental health. My A.C.T. Series is not art therapy. It is a blend, balance, and engagement of spirit, soul, and body. The practice and definition of Creative Spiritual Transformation© can be explained this way. "*It is in this place of "creative therapy" that we can encounter truth, gaining mental clarity and peace of mind while experiencing deep fulfillment. You become so engrossed in what you are doing that you are operating on a level and in a flow that can bring spirit, mind, and body wholeness and wellness. The result is what I call Creative Spiritual Transformation©.*"

Artistic expression quiets our minds, stirs our imagination, and engages our spirit. In this we yield to the Holy Spirit, allowing Him to connect to our heavenly Father. It becomes an avenue for restoring, renewing, and reviving us, ultimately resulting in freedom and whole person Creative Spiritual Transformation©. This is a place of healing and freedom.

Artistic practice allows us to come to a resting place in our mind while being fully awake. You'll be amazed at what can happen when you choose to "Paint the Promise." In 2015, much of my art reflected a deeply broken spirit as I processed decades of emotional and physical pain. One might not have recognized it as brokenness because I chose not to glorify it. I recognized the pain but painted the promise instead. I chose to paint His promises. My work reflected healing, beauty, and life. Art doesn't have to be dark even in our darkest days. When we engage with Holy Spirit and yield to the process, beauty truly does come from our ashes. Light begins to shine through and life comes forth.

The kingdom we carry within us should reflect the King of that kingdom. The heart and nature of our King should be released and recognized in all we do, even our art! We have to create a space where those pains and traumas become a memory or even a memorial, remove them as a block to our destiny, and move on with our journey to wholeness. This is why we recognize the pain, process it with Him, and grab hold of a promise to paint. The pain skews our perception and blocks our destiny. What we choose to focus on matters. It forms thinking habits and creates new pathways in our brains, manifesting either in a positive or negative outcome. Being vigilant in our focus and recognition will lead us to freedom and help us remain free. Remember, recognition can be our greatest ammunition when acted upon and partnered with the Word of God.

It is important that, in seasons of deeply needing the intervention of the Lord, we do not forsake the secret place. We must take time to seek Him and engage with the Holy Spirit in all that we are doing. It is important for all, not just artists, to fill our creative wells and then pour them out. How we cultivate our life with Him out of the workplace or studio space will result in amazing things in those places when we return. As I continue to walk this journey, I keep the following scripture close in mind to remind me that it is only by His Spirit that I am able to do all things.

> *"Not by might, nor by power, but by my Spirit,"* says the LORD *of hosts.*
>
> —Zechariah 4:6, NASB

Application

Pray Ephesians 1:15-23 often asking the Holy Spirit to awaken your spiritual senses. Keep a journal near you when you are creating or gathering inspiration. Record the things you feel, hear, and see with both your physical and spiritual eyes and ears. Look for these four key spiritual and creative growth components that come from the Spirit of wisdom and knowledge.

Inspiration—Idea
Revelation—Understanding
Instruction—Wisdom
Motivation—Ability

Freedom Key

Recognize the pain, allow Holy Spirit to help you process it, and grab hold of a promise. Believe the promise, meditate on it, and apply it to your words and art. Find your creative secret place. Worship in song or dance, or take a walk-in nature with Him, and see how it fuels your work. Believe and expect the Healer to come!

Reflect and Record in Your Journal

Have you experienced a time when you felt like you were engaging in divine flow or reaped benefits from creative expression? Describe the experience and anything you may have gained from it.

Prayer Empowerment

Heavenly Father, I surrender my mind, will, and emotions to you. I release any hurt that I may be harboring and choose to forgive so I may be released and prepared to receive healing. I repent for allowing myself to glorify the pain in my life in any way and diminishing your ability to heal me. Thank you for the gift of creativity and the ability to connect with you as I engage with the Holy Spirit. I surrender my creative gifts back to you. Awaken my spiritual senses so I may receive inspiration, revelation, instruction and motivation to use my gifts in a greater way to bring wholeness to my life and to glorify you. Help me to remember that it is not by my gifts alone, by might, nor by power, but by Your Spirit I am healed and led even in my creative practice. Help me to recognize the pain but choose to paint the promise. Use my gifts for your glory, my joy, and the good of the world. I want to reflect you in all that I do. I ask this in the name of Jesus. Amen.

Chapter 19
THE ART OF KINTSUGI

Mend Them with Gold!

I love the springtime when new blooms break through the ground. From my studio window I had the perfect view of a circle of yellow daffodils as they came to life after a dreary winter. I was content in my corner of the world creating art and drinking in the beautiful daffodils; but reality called, and I would have to emerge from my safe place. In April 2015 I was battling fear and anxiety, and facing society was just too much some days; but the Lord gave me comfort with one verse. As my heart rate would rise and my breathing become shallow, He said, "Trust Me. Do not remember the former things. See, I am doing a new thing!" Immediately peace came and I was able to face the day. He would continue to speak this verse of Isaiah 43 to me time and time again as fear would try to cripple me. He was restoring my peace, but it didn't come easily. As fear relentlessly pounded at the door of my mind, I leaned on His voice in this season like I never had before. His voice was my lifeline!

One morning I was leaving the house and, as I backed out of the driveway, the daffodils caught my eye. Two were completely broken off and lying on the ground; their stems had been bent past the breaking point. I had somewhere to be, but the sight of the damaged flowers stopped me in my tracks. They were too beautiful to let them go to waste. Their life had been cut short, literally. I got out of the car and picked up the daffodils. I laid them on my thigh and looked at how beautiful they were. One was still a closed bloom with the protective coating around its petals and the other was a partially opened bloom. I put them in the water bottle I had in the car and headed out.

When I returned home, I put the blooms in a small vase of water and set them on my art table. They measured about four to six inches high. I was intrigued by these two flowers whose life had been cut short. A few days went by and I began to feel that I needed to preserve them, so I decided to paint them. I challenged my usual method and wondered how to make the art unique and piece them back together, preserve them on a canvas, and give them a solid foundation. I took three pieces of watercolor paper and joined them together from the backside with adhesive, then I began to sketch the flowers on the front. I became obsessed with saving these flower remnants. I was perplexed by my own endeavor, but I kept following the path of my heart. I finished the sketch and brought them to life with watercolors. The three-piece creation sat on my desk for weeks as I contemplated what to do with it next. Eventually the idea came. I prepped the background of a canvas with a wash of soft acrylic colors and then splattered some vibrant inks on what would be a platform for the flowers. Then I decoupaged my mended flowers onto the canvas, giving them a place to rest and firmly attaching them to a new foundation. The project felt complete.

I found it interesting that in this season God was mending my own heart of past brokenness. I believed the daffodils were simply a prophetic expression of love that the Father wanted me to see and experience. But more than that, He wanted me to be a part of mending the flowers. As I used my gift to create something peaceful and beautiful, He used my gift to bring healing to my own heart. He was healing me in the secret place with my gift.

Something amazing began to happen after this. I started to put gold in my work. It was like no work was complete without gold in it. I began seeing images circulating on the Internet of Japanese repaired pottery and received messages from friends about *kintsugi*.

A close friend sent me a picture with an explanation of the art and said, "Dee, I believe this is what you and your ministry do for people. This is what your words and actions are doing." She was referring to the *mending of brokenness*. I was becoming a vessel that ushered in mending the broken and restoring the ruins of other people's heart and life, ultimately bringing them into a place of peace and wholeness.

Until this time in my life, Japanese art did not appeal to me so I didn't know very much about it. I was more of a Monet and Vincent van Gogh girl. But this caught my attention and I knew it was a message from the Lord. I began to read and learn about *kintsugi* and wondered how to apply it to my art. I began to wonder, "Is this my creative kingdom assignment?"

It was six months later when God gave me another message in line with this idea of peace, mending, and wholeness as my ministry. One morning I was meditating on His word and He said, "You are to blaze a path to peace for others, but you cannot take them there if you do not possess peace yourself." It was at that moment that my perspective began to shift about myself and my purpose in the kingdom. I saw that my suffering and struggles all those years were about to be used for His glory. From that point on, I began to pursue peace and vowed to create an atmosphere in my home of love for my family and all who entered. I would house peace and carry it to everyone I encountered.

There is a transformational power in experiencing something that can't be taught through books. We can't give out what we do not have; and if we try, it will not achieve the full effect. When you walk through trials with victory and learn from them, your experience has the potential of being someone else's hope and key to freedom.

What Is Kintsugi?

Kintsugi is the centuries-old Japanese art of fixing broken pottery with a special lacquer that has been dusted with powdered gold, silver, or platinum. It dates back to the fifteenth century and means "the mending of brokenness." *Kin* means "gold" and *tsugi* means "joinery," and is pronounced kin-sue-gee. It is derived from *kinsukuroi*, which means "golden repair." This method takes something broken and transforms it into something beautiful with seams of gold in the cracks of ceramic ware. The veins of gold set it apart and give a unique appearance to the piece. This repair method celebrates each artifact's unique history by emphasizing its fractures and breaks instead of hiding or disguising them. *Kintsugi* often makes the repaired piece even more beautiful than the original form, revitalizing it with new life.

According to legend, the craft began when Japanese shogun Ashikaga Yoshimasa sent a cracked *chawan*—or tea bowl—back to China for repair. Upon its return, Yoshimasa was displeased to find that it had been mended with unsightly metal staples. This motivated contemporary craftsmen to find an alternative, aesthetically pleasing method of repair; and *kintsugi* was born.

Since its conception, *kintsugi* has been heavily influenced by philosophical ideas. The practice is related to the Japanese philosophy of *wabi-sabi*, which calls for seeing beauty in the flawed or imperfect. The repair method was also born from the Japanese feeling of *mottainai*, which expresses regret when something is wasted, as well as *mushin*, the acceptance of change. (Mymodernmet.com and Wikipedia)

So why me and why *kintsugi*? I believe it was a way the Lord could show me visually what He does within us. He gathers up our broken messes and shattered pieces, and, through the Holy Spirit, mends them with his special lacquer of love, a supernatural healing balm. The Lord replaces our heart with His upon our acceptance of salvation in Him; but healing our fragmented lives often comes later. The broken object or remnants have to be handled with the utmost care. Every shard is valuable; and He needs us to surrender every piece to Him so He can finish His masterpiece in us. He would only choose the best for us because we are valuable to Him; that is the reason for the gold. The gold is for His glory.

I met with Him in prayer to intercede for the burdens and brokenness of others, especially women suffering like I had, post-abortive, depressed, defeated, and depleted. The words "paint the promise" began to echo in my head. I continued to seek His direction for my art. I didn't want to just paint my message, I wanted to paint His message. One day as I drove home from my studio, I said to Him, "I want a story; what is the story you want me to tell with my art?" He clearly and quickly said, "Mend them with gold! You already have the story." He went on to explain His greater desires for *our* art: "You are to blaze a path to healing and peace with your work. Help mend their broken spirits with your heart and art. Paint the promise! Paint the promise! Continue to paint the promise in your pieces with my Spirit and the art of *kintsugi*!"

Then Holy Spirit reminded me of Psalm 147:3: "He heals the brokenhearted and binds up their wounds." This was the Spirit of the Lord in the art of *kintsugi*! It was clear what my assignment was to be as a kingdom artist: to display His glory, mend with gold, and release beauty and His promises in the earth! I saw Isaiah 61 all over my ministry and my art and I ran with it.

As time went on, I began to wonder if I was *really* mending brokenness with my art and writings. I was doing what the Lord told me, but thoughts plagued me once again that diminished my work and credibility as an artist. I was in a new fight for my life. I needed to stay free and walk the call that I knew, without a shadow of a doubt, God had placed on my life.

Holy Spirit reminded me to take the thoughts and comments captive and replace them with God's truth. I must have been doing something right because the lies and arrows came and tried to throw me off course and destroy me. I stuck to my guns and kept on speaking His truth, painting flowers, and mending them with gold.

In 2017 I read Makoto Fujimura's book *Culture Care: Reconnecting with Beauty for Our Common Life.* Fujimura, a man of the Christian faith, boldly proclaims his beliefs in his speeches, books, and artwork. He is a "way maker" for artists who desire to do the same and he gave me courage to speak out about art and faith in my life. Fujimura, an internationally renowned Japanese-American artist and author, saw a need to care for his culture, especially after the tragedy of 9/11 in America.

He founded Culture Care and implemented the idea of generative thinking. Culture Care is about caring and providing for the soul of our culture by reconnecting others to beauty for our common life. Maybe you're wondering what beauty can do for a culture. The answer is *everything*. Jesus alone was the most beautiful gift ever given to humanity. Expressing the Father's heart through our gifts can change the world. The beauty displayed through our gifts reflects the characteristics of God.

It's true that art is not practical, but it is necessary for the soul. Art can be a generative force for life when portrayed properly. Fujimura states, "Artists ultimately can reveal new facets of human flourishing even in the midst of tragedy or horror, pointing toward hope and meaning. Our arts and conversations should point toward beauty and healing" (*Culture Care: Reconnecting with Beauty for Our Common Life*).

That was exactly what the Lord told me to do. I was caring for the soul of my culture through the message of *kintsugi* in my work, partnered with the Gospel of Jesus Christ. As artists and leaders in the Christian faith, we need to see, listen, give, and guide with our art and words, releasing beauty and generating life. Fujimura's book resonated deeply with me and gave me courage to continue to paint the promise regardless of what society had to say about it. I would not compromise my gift, my faith, or the assignments that were given to me.

Redemption in Chicago – Not Just an Art Show!

In 2018 God aligned my life with two prominent, internationally known voices in the art world and emotional wellness arena. Sergio and Yanina Gomez are founders of Art NXT Level and operate 33 Contemporary Art Gallery in Chicago. Sergio is an art mentor and curator. I participated in a webinar they hosted. Immediately following the webinar, I received a phone call from Sergio asking how he could help me. I was surprised and impressed. I had never received a phone call from the host of a webinar. We had a great conversation and became fast art friends! I quickly joined their art mentoring group. It was an answer to a prayer I had prayed just a few months prior asking the Lord to send someone to help me take my art to the next level.

One month into the mentoring group, Sergio announced that they would be hosting an exclusive Art NXT Level self-portrait show at their gallery in Chicago. I was excited and a little freaked out at the same time. I wasn't a portrait artist; I was a nature and floral artist. He said it didn't have to be a literal portrait. We could use anything that represented

THE ART OF KINTSUGI

us. The wheels of creativity began to turn. Immediately I saw white magnolias!

I began to sketch out and plan the painting. It would be a triptych representing three phases of me and my life. As I prepped the canvases, I immediately knew what colors they were to be: teal, white, and gold. I wanted to incorporate *kintsugi* into my personal mending story.

I started with a closed white bloom that was full of promise and had the purity of innocence with its whole life ahead of it. From there I moved to an open bloom that was supported by leaves; but it had lost its innocence and was colorless. This second bloom was war-torn and scarred. You could see cracks in the core of the bloom and the delicate petals marred by the storms of life. I wanted the bloom to show a void of purpose and joy, with a transparent look that represented vulnerability.

As I painted these pieces late into the night, I could feel liquid love flowing over my heart as scenes of my life flashed before my eyes. I cried as I painted. Tears often accompany my secret place works because I feel what the Holy Spirit is accomplishing.

The third and final bloom came out like a racehorse sprinting at the end of a race, making a comeback from behind to cross the finish line. I moved the pure white and ivory paint tinted with pearlescent shimmer across the vibrant teal backdrop. The petals, still supported by strong branches and leaves, began to extend and display themselves fully in bloom. I traced the cracks of the core and the restored petals and watched as the fine liquid gold paint filled the crevices. The mending was almost complete. The core and one petal remained translucent, like a veil, as a reminder that we have to remain vulnerable with ourselves and God—and keep our hearts open to Him—so He can continue to reach and refine us. The only way that happens is by humble surrender at the feet of Jesus, in that secret place behind the veil. My self-portrait was complete. A wave of emotion came over me the day I mailed it to Chicago. I couldn't believe that my work would be shown in a prestigious big city gallery. God knew this day would come.

I booked my flight to attend the opening in July 2018, more than twenty years since I had last been to Chicago. It was a prophetic act of redemption to show my art in the city where my life had taken a tragic turn. Chicago was the very place that Satan stole life from my womb, twice. Chicago was the city where my first two children went to be with the Lord through the act of abortion.

Opening night came with all sorts of emotions including excitement and the satisfaction of victory. I saw my work on the wall at the gallery with people looking at it. I wasn't sure if I wanted to shout for joy or cry. I just felt like something had been restored and completed in me and in the spiritual realm of my life. No one in that room knew my story, nor did they realize the true meaning of the art they were looking at. My triptych, titled "Mended," was a message to Satan. He thought he was going to destroy me, but God took what was meant for harm and turned it around for good. It was also a message to give others hope that they, too, can be mended, no matter what the circumstances are.

As I sat in the middle of the gallery that night with Yanina, I told her how thankful I was for the opportunity that she and Sergio had given me. I didn't tell her details that night, but I did tell her how important it was that I was there with my art because God had just brought something full circle in my life. The chapter from the beginning of my adult life with the heartbreak of broken relationships and sin of abortion was now closed. He had given me an opportunity to use my artistic gift to fully heal my heart and send out a prophetic message of victory. It was finished and now I could move forward with my new assignments in the kingdom. This, no doubt, was a divine moment. It was a moment for the cross of Christ to be enforced and for God to be glorified in my life.

For decades I fought the lie of shame, believing that I was not worthy to have children of my own. Now thirty years after the initial abortions I see the fruit of mercy and forgiveness and how he is still restoring and redeeming everything in my life. My husband and I have been blessed with two beautiful and amazing children who love God and have dedicated their life to serving Him faithfully. If that is not an act of redemption, I do not know what is.

It might have seemed petty to pick up and save those broken daffodils that day, but I was caring for the culture around me. They were more than flowers; they were a message to my heart and to the world. I mended the brokenness and found a message of hope in the midst of it—a message that healed me and set me on the path of my purpose as an artist. It was a message of *kintsugi*, and of Isaiah 61 proclaiming the gift and promise of our Lord Jesus.

As one who has suffered—soulfully and physically imprisoned—I count it an honor to co-labor with the Lord to bind up the brokenhearted and bring freedom to the captives by releasing peace, joy, and hope. Together we all can help rebuild ancient ruins and restore the places long devastated.

As I recall the journey of my life and the path of this book, it is clear that God's message is one of love and restoration, for our good and for His glory. His will is that none should perish. Above all, it is His desire that we seek Him first, putting no other thing before Him. He can take you from wandering to found, from pain to promise, and from struggle to peace. He did it for me and I am confident He will do it for you. As you surrender all of your valuable and broken pieces, let go of the prize they have become and allow Him to replace the pain with the promise of Himself.

He has been faithful through it all, divinely orchestrating my life from the moment I encountered Him in the Catholic church to the day I found the daffodils and beyond. It is my prayer that you have heard His whisper and found healing and freedom in the pages of this book. Can you see Him divinely orchestrating your life? If so, are you following His lead?

It is my greatest hope that you are more aware of Him and are on your way to housing a restored heart, a renewed soul, and a revived body in order to live out your days transformed and free in the goodness of God for His purposes. The day I gave up and surrendered my prized pieces to Him became my day of true freedom. *My purpose may have come out of my pain, but it is not my greatest treasure. Instead my pain pushed me to find my greatest treasure: Him.* I was now experiencing the promise of Isaiah 61. He rebuilt the ruins of my heart, adorned me with beauty from within, smeared me with the oil of joy, and clothed me in a garment of praise. I was now able—transformed and free—to display His glory as I co-labor with Him the rest of my days, carrying out the promise of healing and hope to others.

I love to show my art and speak about the process and meaning behind the pieces. It is an honor to share the promises that I have painted straight from the Father's heart. You can view the artwork "Mended" along with others at my website www.dionnewhiteart.com.

Do you want to blaze a path to peace in your own life? Consider The Art of Freedom creative companion course A.C.T. ~ Awake. Create. Transform! to awaken, establish, and engage your unique identity and creative gifts, becoming a healed and whole artist of purpose. Available now at www.dionnewhiteart.com to learn more.

Take the online **Freedom Zone© Assessment** now to see where you are in your journey of freedom and transformation.

Visit www.theartoffreedombook.com for the assessment, further details and offers. Receive free PDF downloads from the book to start your personal journey today. ***Don't put freedom and transformation off another day!***

ENDNOTES

Fujimura, Makoto., and Mark Labberton. *Culture Care: Reconnecting with Beauty for Our Common Life.* New York City; International Arts Movement and the Fujimura Institute;, 2017.

Gregory, Susan. *The Daniel Fast: Feed Your Soul, Strengthen Your Spirit, and Renew Your Body.* Carol Stream: Tyndale Momentum, 2010.

Henderson, Robert. *Operating in the Courts of Heaven: Granting God the Legal Rights to Fulfill His Passion.* Waco: Robert Henderson Ministries, 2016.

Leaf, Caroline. Controlling Your Toxic Thoughts. https://drleaf.com/blogs/news.

------. *The Perfect You.* Nashville: Thomas Nelson Incorporated, 2017.

------. *Switch On Your Brain.* Nashville: Thomas Nelson Incorporated, 2015

------. *Switch On Your Brain Every Day: 365 Readings for Peak Happiness, Thinking, and Health.* Nashville: Thomas Nelson Incorporated, 2018.

------. *Who Switched Off My Brain?* Nashville: Thomas Nelson Incorporated, 2007

Rubin, Jordan. *The Maker's Diet*. Berkley: New York City, 2005.

Terkeurst, Lysa. *The Best Yes: Making Wise Decisions in the Midst of Endless Demands*. Nashville: Thomas Nelson, 2014.

Thompson, Adam F., and Adrian Bealle. *The Divinity Code to Understanding Your Dreams and Visions*. Destiny Image Publishers: Shippensburg, 2011.

White, Dionne. A.C.T. Series; Awake, Create, Transform. © Anderson, 2020.

White, Dionne. The Art of Freedom Paradigm© Venn Diagram. *The Art of Freedom*, Powell,

Author Academy Elite, 2020.

ABOUT THE AUTHOR

Dionne White is primarily a self-taught Creative. She is an Artist, Teacher, Writer, Mentor, Minister and Creative Coach, working to release beauty and hope to a hurting world. She is dedicated to equipping others in their gifts and longs to see restoration and sustained revival in the culture around her. Dionne is leading others in whole person transformation with her biblically based *Art of Freedom Paradigm*© teaching, causing them to believe for a different outcome rather than the "cards they were dealt". This is the mission behind her ministry, to share the hope of Jesus and bring restoration and transformation to all.

She is an award winning and nationally showing inspirational kintsugi Painter, spiritual and artistic Content Creator, Podcaster and emerging prophetic voice in the body of Christ. Dionne's teaching and ministry approach is fresh, fiery, fun and practical. She is the Founder, Artist, and Voice of Mini Masterpiece Monday, *Painting the Promise*© instructional art videos, Developer of *The A.C.T. Series; Awake. Create. Transform. Kingdom Artist of Purpose Curriculum* and host of *Creative Conversations with Dionne White Podcast*© (found on your major podcast platforms Apple, Spotify, Google Podcasts, Anchor, Breaker, Castbox, Radio Public, Pocket Casts and Overcast). Dionne also founded Infused Intercession, an online prophetic ministry group where she gathers, equips, empowers, and activates others in prophetic intercession and spiritual gifts ministry.

Dionne has spoken for Aglow International, Greenville, SC Lighthouse Chapter as well as Clemson University, collaborating with local campus organization Tigers Together for mental health and suicide awareness. Her prophetic and inspirational content has been published with Spirit Fuel, The Elijah List and JewelsMagazine.org.

Dionne is a NE Ohio native. She and her husband, Will, have two children Asher and Anna and currently resides in South Carolina.

Contact or Invite Dionne to minister, speak or teach @ www.dionnewhiteart.com or www.theartoffreedombook.com via the contact form.

A NOTE TO CREATIVES

To my fellow Creatives,

There comes a time when *what you do* reveals *who you are*. God's call for you as an artist reveals *who you were created to be*. God does everything with purpose. Artists have a purpose and when He reveals *His* purpose for you in creating with Him, you realize it's not just to do what you love; it's to do what you love with a purpose, His purpose, releasing heaven on earth. What you do with Him should bring change for the better. Commit to creating art that generates life and cares for the soul of yourself and the culture around you releasing His beauty. I have created a kingdom artist curriculum to help you develop as an artist of intuition and purpose. The Awake ~ Create ~ Transform© Creative Curriculum will bring you closer to the Lord and develop your relationship with Holy Spirit through practical and spiritual application. Founded on kingdom principles with biblical truths partnered with your gift(s) and the Holy Spirit will allow you to release heaven on earth and experience Creative Spiritual Transformation©. It is my great honor to put a kingdom arts resource into your hands that will generate life in you and the world around you. Let us overcome evil with good. (*–Romans 12:21)* Let us display His glory!

"May we always be willing to present a bouquet of flowers, even to an artist – or a culture – who may not yet know that they desire beauty." Makoto Fujimura – Culture Care

Creatively in Him,
Dionne

Do you want to find peace, purpose, and greater fulfillment with your creative and spiritual gifts?

Available Now for Digital Download,
A.C.T. ONE of the **A.C.T. Series–**
Awake. Create. Transform!

A Biblically based creative curriculum to establish and fuel your personal creative journey of becoming an artist of purpose.

A.C.T. ONE -
Awake, available now at
www.dionnewhiteart.com

A.C.T. TWO -
Create, available
January of 2021

A.C.T. THREE -
Transform, available
January of 2022

Join The Art of Freedom and A.C.T. Movements. **Invite Dionne to speak, teach or minister at your next ministry, school, or creative event.** Visit www.dionnewhiteart.com to contact and learn more.

www.ingramcontent.com/pod-product-compliance
Lightning Source LLC
LaVergne TN
LVHW021716060526
838200LV00050B/2689